Illustrated Short Stories in English

Steven Reeder, Oksun Kang

Illustrator, Hyosun An

Shinasa

Text Notes

All stories are offered on the public domain.

Edgar Allan Poe: "The Cask of Amontillado," from the November 1846 issue of *Godey's Lady's Book.*

Mark Twain: *The Adventures of Tom Sawyer*, "Chapter 2," from the 1876 novel.

Kate Chopin: "The Story of the Hour," from the January 5, 1895 edition of *St. Louis Life.*

O. Henry: "The Gift of the Magi," from the 1906 short story collection *The Four Million.*

Oscar Wilde: "The Happy Prince," from 1888 short story collection *The Happy Prince and Other Tales.*

James Joyce: "Araby," from the 1914 short story collection *Dubliners.*

Saki: "The Open Window," from the 1914 short story collection *Beasts and Superbeasts.*

Virginia Woolf: "A Haunted House," from the 1944 short story collection *A Haunted House and Other Short Stories.*

Guy de Maupassant: "The Diamond Necklace," from *Original Short Stories—Volume 4*. Translated by A.E. Henderson. Offered Kindly on the public domain.

Leo Tolstoy: "Three Questions," from the 1898 short story collection *What Men Live By, and Other Tales*. Translated by L. and A. Maude.

The Essentials: A Prologue

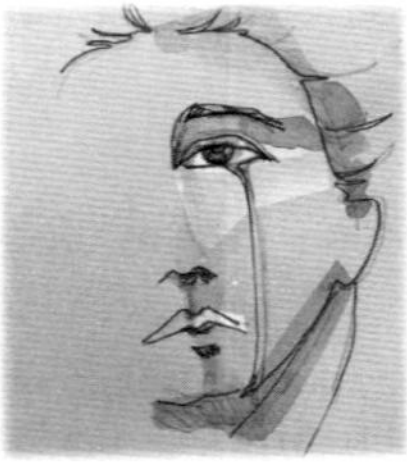

Reading is a skill all second-language learners need to master. Once a student has learned to understand the text, the fun part is about to begin. The student then needs to dive into the text to gather a net of meaning. If reading were just the understanding of the story, then literature as a branch of study would not exist. In fact, it would be on the same level as most Hollywood movies—just hollow stories with no depth. Fortunately, literature authors are skilled in their craft, and readers need to be just as informed.

The artistic nature of short stories often makes them difficult to read. Many do not follow the conventional beginning, middle, and end style most are familiar with in fiction. The language is often poetic, and the choice of words is deliberate, making it difficult for second language readers to thoroughly enjoy a story. What should be a wonderful appreciation of the written word often turns into frustration and boredom.

The purpose of this book is to remedy this problem by making the stories more accessible to ESL readers. To fully immerse literature students in each story, we have introduced the authors with a brief biography that can help the reader understand the environment and situations in which the short stories were written. Since the stories are from the late 19th and early 20th century, the language and style may be harder to comprehend fully compared to modern texts. For this reason, I have included a brief synopsis of each story. With the basic plot firmly in mind, the reader can focus more on language and the style in which it was written for a fuller and more pleasurable reading experience. Also, many of the words and expressions that are archaic and hard to find in most dictionaries have been included at the end of each story with simple explanations to fit the context of their usage. Not only that, but also to facilitate a greater and deeper meaning from the stories, study questions are offered at the end of each chapter to encourage a second or third reading and even as a basis for essay questions. And finally, a glossary of common literary terms can be found in the appendix to introduce students to the various techniques of reading, writing, and studying literature.

The choice of authors was rather simple. We chose writers whose works are offered on the public domain. This means their copyrights have not been renewed and have expired sixty years after their deaths. We also wanted to have an equal representation of American and British writers, four each, along with two non-English writers. We felt a balance of different literary genres written by the pioneers of each genre would give a student a sense of the different styles of writing offered in the English language: psychological horror by Edgar Allan Poe; feminism by Kate Chopin; allegory by O. Henry; bildungsroman by Mark Twain; fairy tale by Oscar Wilde; literary myth by James Joyce; irony by Saki; flash fiction by Virginia Woolf; historical fiction by Guy de Maupassant; and a parable by Leo Tolstoy.

We hope that students will find these selections as enjoyable as we do. Nothing of value is ever gained easily, and getting to know these stories well will prove to be difficult. But with effort and patience, these readings will stay within our memories for the rest of our lives. So, sit back, read, and let the story overcome your emotions; let the tales envelop you, allowing you to feel at home in these foreign accounts of faraway people and places.

Steven Reeder
Kyungsung University

Contents

MP3 files can be downloaded at publisher's homepage: www.shinasa.co.kr

American Short Stories

Edgar Allan Poe: The Cask of Amontillado (1846)
Mark Twain: The Adventures of Tom Sawyer, Chapter 2 (1876)
Kate Chopin: The Story of an Hour (1894)
O. Henry: The Gift of the Magi (1905)

I

THE CASK OF AMONTILLADO

by Edgar Allan Poe (1846, The Northeast: Boston, Massachusetts)

- Introduction of the Author
- Synopsis
- Text
- Words & Idioms
- Study Questions

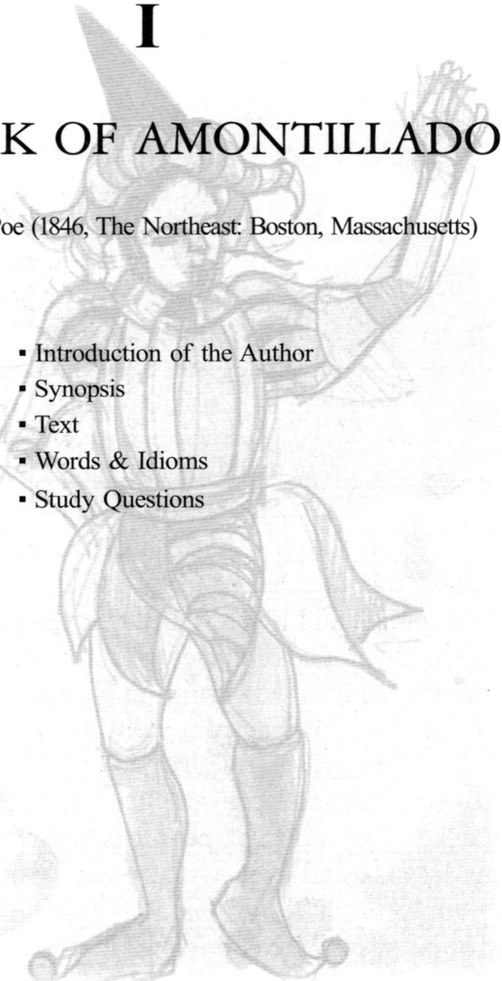

Introduction of the Author: Edgar Allan Poe (1809-1849)

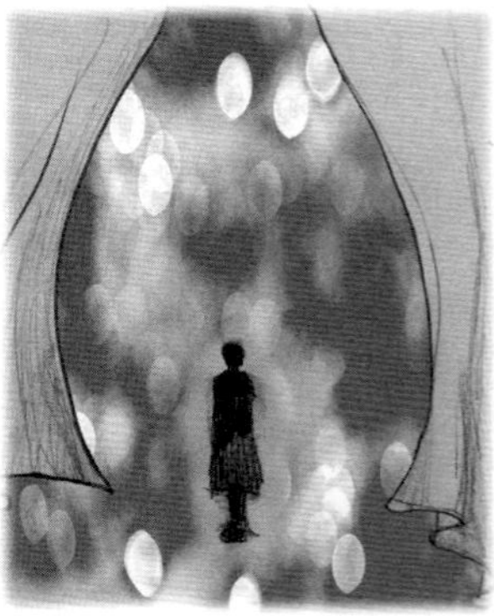

Born January 19, 1809, Edgar Allan Poe was the son of two poor traveling theater actors, a profession that was not respected at the time. Edgar's father, David Poe, often appeared drunk on stage and was a notorious drinker and even abandoned his family when Edgar was two years old. A year later his mother died violently of tuberculosis, an event that traumatized him into his later years.

Edgar was then taken in by the Allans, though never legally adopted, and given the best education, which included five years in England. Poe entered the University of Virginia where he fell into debt through abundant gambling. When he refused to pay back the debt, he was expelled. His expulsion from university shamed the Allans deeply enough to disown him and prevent his marriage to Sarah Elmira Royster. Facing a dismal, penniless future, Poe enlisted in the army in 1827 and even wrote poems. His first book of poetry appeared in *Tamerlane and Other Poems*, a style that borrowed heavily from the English poet Lord Byron.

After being honorably discharged from West Point, a top military academy, for refusing to follow orders, Poe turned to writing full time and contributed to several magazines from 1835 to 1843. During this time, he published some of his best-known stories. He moved to Baltimore and lived with his widowed Aunt and her daughter Virginia Clem.

Poe was the center of several scandals when his drinking and drug use became well known. He also caused a stir when he married his cousin Virginia, who was only 13 at the time. Five years later, she died of tuberculosis after bursting a blood vessel and becoming an invalid. The drugs and drinking nearly destroyed Poe after the death of his wife. However, he still maintained legitimacy as a writer, an adept literary critic, and by publishing *The Murders in the Rue Morgue* (1841), which became the precursor to the great works of mystery that followed, especially Sir Arthur Conan Doyle's Sherlock Holmes character. Many critics consider Poe to be the creator of the short story form, though this is still much in debate. His most famous short story is *The Fall of the House of Usher* (1839).

By 1845, Poe had moved to New York where he penned his now famous poem "The Raven." His erratic behavior and bouts of madness led to his attempting suicide by overdosing on the drug laudanum. It was during this time he penned the superb tale of cold revenge *The Cask of Amontillado* (1846). Since Poe became associated with tales of the macabre and was well known for being a drug addict and alcoholic, many readers thought the dark characters of his stories were somewhat autobiographical.

After years of such physical and mental abuse—the death of his wife, and abject poverty—Poe was found unconscious in the gutter on October 3, 1849. He stayed in this state for four more days before he died. He is now fondly remembered as the father of the detective story and modern horror.

Synopsis

The narrator, Montresor, is deeply upset by all the insults and injuries he has suffered from Fortunato. Though he never tells the reader what these injuries are, or if they are indeed worth the horror he inflicts on Fortunato, Montresor shows that he is cold and calculating in his revenge. Having dismissed all his servants, and preparing bricks and mortar in advance, Montresor finds Fortunato at a time of festival and begins to tempt his unwary prey into following him. He tells Fortunato that he has stored some very rare wine in the cellar beneath his manor. He uses reverse psychology to trick Fortunato into following him. Ironically, Fortunato is dressed as a fool for the festival, which is how Montresor views him. Furthermore, Montresor's darkness worsens when he states concern for Fortunato's health and well-being, an obvious lie in contrast to the way he murders him later.

Giving his hapless prey more liquor to numb his senses, Montresor leads Fortunato deep within the crypt. At the farthest reaches, they come to a narrow nook, where he has Fortunato enter to find the rare Amontillado. Inside, Montresor chains him to the wall and starts to trap Fortunato inside by laying bricks in the opening and sealing them with mortar. Fortunato starts to sober to his situation and screams in horror. Montresor screams back, louder and more insanely until Fortunato becomes quiet. With all but the last brick in place, Montresor throws the torch in to see the response of his victim and wishes him to rest in peace before sealing the nook, roughly the size of a coffin, forever.

Text

The thousand injuries of Fortunato I had borne as I best could, but when he ventured upon insult, I vowed revenge. You, who so well know the nature of my soul, will not suppose, however, that I gave utterance to a threat. At length I would be avenged; this was a point definitively settled—but the very definitiveness with which it was resolved precluded the idea of risk. I must not only punish, but punish with impunity. A wrong is unredressed when retribution overtakes its redresser. It is equally unredressed when the avenger fails to make himself felt as such to him who has done the wrong.

It must be understood that neither by word nor deed had I given Fortunato cause to doubt my good will. I continued as was my wont, to smile in his face, and he did not perceive that my smile now was at the thought of his immolation.

He had a weak point--this Fortunato -- although in other regards he was a man to be respected and even feared. He prided himself on his connoisseurship in wine. Few Italians have the true virtuoso spirit. For the most part their enthusiasm is adopted to suit the time and opportunity to practise imposture upon the British and Austrian millionairs. In painting and gemmary, Fortunato, like his countrymen, was a quack, but in the matter of old wines he was sincere. In this respect I did

not differ from him materially; I was skilful in the Italian vintages myself, and bought largely whenever I could.

It was about dusk, one evening during the supreme madness of the carnival season, that I encountered my friend. He accosted me with excessive warmth, for he had been drinking much. The man wore motley. He had on a tight-fitting parti-striped dress and his head was surmounted by the conical cap and bells. I was so pleased to see him, that I thought I should never have done wringing his hand.

I said to him -- "My dear Fortunato, you are luckily met. How remarkably well you are looking today! But I have received a pipe of what passes for Amontillado, and I have my doubts."

"How?" said he, "Amontillado? A pipe? Impossible? And in the middle of the carnival?"

"I have my doubts," I replied; "and I was silly enough to pay the full Amontillado price without consulting you in the matter. You were not to be found, and I was fearful of losing a bargain."

"Amontillado!"

"I have my doubts."

"Amontillado!"

"And I must satisfy them."

"Amontillado!"

"As you are engaged, I am on my way to Luchesi. If any one has a critical turn, it is he. He will tell me" --

"Luchesi cannot tell Amontillado from Sherry."

"And yet some fools will have it that his taste is a match for your own."

"Come let us go."

"Whither?"

"To your vaults."

"My friend, no; I will not impose upon your good nature. I perceive you have an engagement Luchesi" --

"I have no engagement; come."

"My friend, no. It is not the engagement, but the severe cold with which I perceive you are afflicted. The vaults are insufferably damp. They are encrusted with nitre."

"Let us go, nevertheless. The cold is merely nothing. Amontillado! You have been imposed upon; and as for Luchesi, he cannot distinguish Sherry from Amontillado."

Thus speaking, Fortunato possessed himself of my arm. Putting on a mask of black silk and drawing a roquelaire closely about my person, I suffered him to hurry me to my palazzo.

There were no attendants at home; they had absconded to make merry in honour of the time. I had told them that I should not return until the morning and had given them explicit orders not to stir from the house. These orders were sufficient, I well knew, to insure their immediate disappearance, one and all, as soon as my back was turned.

I took from their sconces two flambeaux, and giving one to Fortunato bowed him through several suites of rooms to the archway that led into the vaults. I passed down a long and winding staircase, requesting him to be cautious as he followed. We came at length to the foot of the descent, and stood together on the damp ground of the catacombs of the Montresors.

The gait of my friend was unsteady, and the bells upon his cap jingled as he strode.

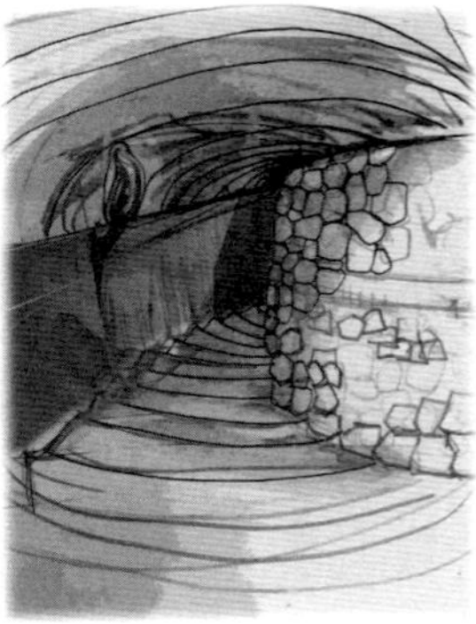

"The pipe," said he.

"It is farther on," said I; "but observe the white webwork which gleams from these cavern walls."

He turned towards me and looked into my eyes with two filmy orbs that distilled the rheum of intoxication.

"Nitre?" he asked, at length

"Nitre," I replied. "How long have you had that cough!"

"Ugh! ugh! ugh! -- ugh! ugh! ugh! -- ugh! ugh! ugh! -- ugh! ugh! ugh! -- ugh! ugh! ugh!

My poor friend found it impossible to reply for many minutes.

"It is nothing," he said, at last.

"Come," I said, with decision, We will go back; your health is precious. You are rich, respected, admired, beloved; you are happy as once I was. You are a man to be missed. For me it is no matter. We will go back; you will be ill and I cannot be responsible. Besides, there is Luchesi" --

"Enough," he said; "the cough is a mere nothing; it will not kill me. I shall not die of a cough."

"True -- true," I replied; "and, indeed, I had no intention of alarming you unnecessarily -- but you should use all proper caution. A draught of this Medoc will defend us from the damps."

Here I knocked off the neck of a bottle which I drew from a long row of its fellows that lay upon the mould.

"Drink," I said, presenting him the wine.

He raised it to his lips with a leer. He paused and nodded to me familiarly, while his bells jingled.

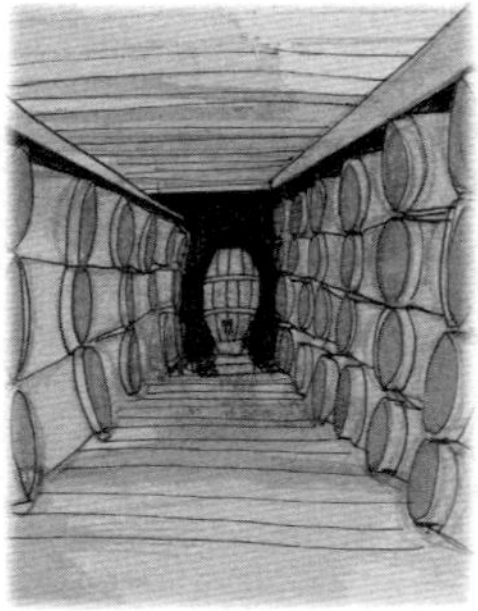

"I drink," he said, "to the buried that repose around us."

"And I to your long life."

He again took my arm and we proceeded.

"These vaults," he said, are extensive."

"The Montresors," I replied, "were a great numerous family."

"I forget your arms."

"A huge human foot d'or, in a field azure; the foot crushes a serpent rampant whose fangs are imbedded in the heel."

"And the motto?"

"*Nemo me impunelacessit.*"

"Good!" he said.

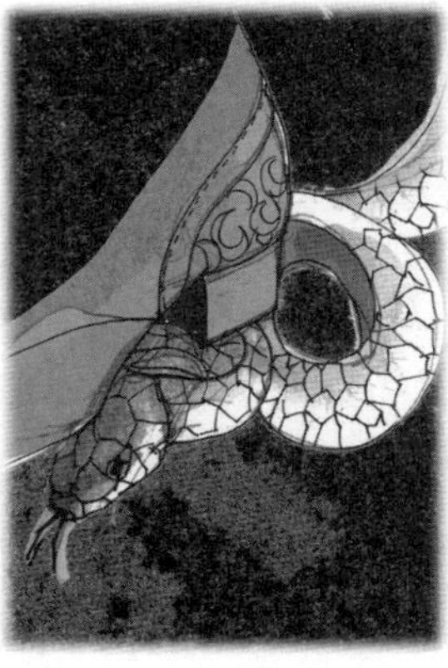

The wine sparkled in his eyes and the bells jingled. My own fancy grew warm with the Medoc. We had passed through walls of piled bones, with casks and puncheons intermingling, into the inmost recesses of the catacombs. I paused again, and this time I made bold to seize Fortunato by an arm above the elbow.

"The nitre!" I said: see it increases. It hangs like moss upon the vaults. We are below the river's bed. The drops of moisture trickle among the bones. Come, we will go back ere it is too late. Your cough" --

"It is nothing" he said; "let us go on. But first, another draught of the Medoc."

I broke and reached him a flagon of De Grave. He emptied it at a breath. His eyes flashed with a fierce light. He laughed and threw the bottle upwards with a gesticulation I did not understand.

I looked at him in surprise. He repeated the movement -- a grotesque one.

"You do not comprehend?" he said.

"Not I," I replied.

"Then you are not of the brotherhood."

"How?"

"You are not of the masons."

"Yes, yes," I said "yes! yes."

"You? Impossible! A mason?"

"A mason," I replied.

"A sign," he said.

"It is this," I answered, producing a trowel from beneath the folds of my roquelaire.

"You jest," he exclaimed, recoiling a few paces. "But let us proceed to the Amontillado."

"Be it so," I said, replacing the tool beneath the cloak, and again offering him my arm. He leaned upon it heavily. We continued our route in search of the Amontillado. We passed through a range of low arches, descended, passed on, and descending again, arrived at a deep crypt, in which the foulness of the air caused our flambeaux rather to glow than flame.

At the most remote end of the crypt there appeared another less spacious. Its walls had been lined with human remains piled to the vault overhead, in the fashion of the great catacombs of Paris. Three sides of this interior crypt were still ornamented in this manner. From the fourth the bones had been thrown down, and lay promiscuously upon the earth, forming at one point a mound of some size. Within the wall thus exposed by the displacing of the bones, we perceived a still interior recess, in depth about four feet, in width three, in height six or seven. It seemed to have been constructed for no especial use in itself, but formed merely the interval between two of the colossal supports of the roof of the catacombs, and was backed by one of their circumscribing walls of solid granite.

It was in vain that Fortunato, uplifting his dull torch, endeavoured to pry into the depths of the recess. Its termination the feeble light did not enable us to see.

"Proceed," I said; "herein is the Amontillado. As for Luchesi" --

"He is an ignoramus," interrupted my friend, as he stepped unsteadily forward, while I followed immediately at his heels. In an instant he had reached the extremity of the niche, and finding his progress arrested by the rock, stood stupidly bewildered. A moment more and I had fettered him to the granite. In its surface were two iron staples, distant from each other about two feet, horizontally. From one of these depended a short chain. from the other a padlock. Throwing the links about his waist, it was but the work of a few seconds to secure it. He was too much astounded to resist. Withdrawing the key I stepped back from the recess.

"Pass your hand," I said, "over the wall; you cannot help feeling the nitre. Indeed it is very damp. Once more let me implore you to return. No? Then I must positively leave you. But I must first render you all the little attentions in my power."

"The Amontillado!" ejaculated my friend, not yet recovered from his astonishment.

"True," I replied; "the Amontillado."

As I said these words I busied myself among the pile of bones of which I have before spoken. Throwing them aside,

I soon uncovered a quantity of building stone and mortar. With these materials and with the aid of my trowel, I began vigorously to wall up the entrance of the niche.

I had scarcely laid the first tier of my masonry when I discovered that the intoxication of Fortunato had in a great measure worn off. The earliest indication I had of this was a low moaning cry from the depth of the recess. It was not the cry of a drunken man. There was then a long and obstinate silence. I laid the second tier, and the third, and the fourth; and then I heard the furious vibrations of the chain. The noise lasted for several minutes, during which, that I might hearken to it with the more satisfaction, I ceased my labours and sat down upon the bones.

When at last the clanking subsided, I resumed the trowel, and finished without interruption the fifth, the sixth, and the seventh tier. The wall was now nearly upon a level with my breast. I again paused, and holding the flambeaux over the mason-work, threw a few feeble rays upon the figure within.

A succession of loud and shrill screams, bursting suddenly from the throat of the chained form, seemed to thrust me violently back. For a brief moment I hesitated -- I trembled. Unsheathing my rapier, I began to grope with it about the recess; but the thought of an instant reassured me. I placed my hand upon the solid fabric of the catacombs, and felt satisfied. I reapproached the wall. I replied to the yells of him who clamoured. I re-echoed -- I aided -- I surpassed them in volume and in strength. I did this, and the clamourer grew still.

It was now midnight, and my task was drawing to a close. I had completed the eighth, the ninth, and the tenth tier. I had finished a portion of the last and the eleventh; there remained but a single stone to be fitted and plastered in. I struggled with its weight; I placed it partially in its destined position. But now there came from out the niche a low laugh that erected the hairs upon my head. It was succeeded by a sad voice, which I had difficulty in recognising as that of the noble Fortunato. The voice said --

"Ha! ha! ha! -- he! he! -- a very good joke indeed -- an excellent jest. We will have many a rich laugh about it at the palazzo -- he! he! he! -- over our wine -- he! he! he!"

"The Amontillado!" I said.

"He! he! he! -- he! he! he! -- yes, the Amontillado. But is it not getting late? Will not they be awaiting us at the palazzo, the Lady Fortunato and the rest? Let us be gone."

"Yes," I said, "let us be gone."

"For the love of God, Montresor!"

"Yes," I said, "for the love of God!"

But to these words I hearkened in vain for a reply. I grew impatient. I called aloud --

"Fortunato!"

No answer. I called again --

"Fortunato!"

No answer still. I thrust a torch through the remaining aperture and let it fall within. There came forth in return only a jingling of the bells. My heart grew sick -- on account of the dampness of the catacombs. I hastened to make an end of my labour. I forced the last stone into its position; I plastered it up. Against the new masonry I reerected the old rampart of bones. For the half of a century no mortal has disturbed them.

In pace requiescat!

Words & Idioms

abscond: (v) to leave rapidly so as not to be seen.
accost: (v) to stand close to a person and talk aggressively or without fear.
Amontillado: (n) a dry, sweet wine (sherry) from Spain.
arms (coat of arms): (n) a family emblem that shows ancestry.
azure: (adj) the color of blue.
cask: (n) a wooden barrel that is used to hold beer or wine.
connoisseurship: (n) a great knowledge or taste for superior things.
definitiveness: (n) conclusiveness or finality
d'or: (French) gold.
ejaculate: (v) to speak quickly and suddenly.
ere: (prep) before.
flambeaux: (n) a torch that is already lit.
gemmary: (n) the skill of cutting of gems.
gesticulation: (n) moving hands for emphasis while speaking; gesturing.
ignoramus: (n) a person who is ignorant.
immolation: (n) killing or destruction.
impunity: (n) to do something without getting caught, punished, or hurt.
***In pace requiescat*:** (Latin) Rest in peace (May his soul not be troubled in death).
mason: (n) a person that builds with bricks, also a secret order of fraternity.
Medoc: (n) a red wine from Bordeaux, France.
mortar: (n) a special type of cement that is used to stick bricks together when building.

motley: (n) the multi-colored clothing worn by a court jester or clown in the Middle Ages.

***Nemo me impunelacessit*:** (Latin) No one assails (attacks) me with impunity (without consequence).

niche: (n) a small closet-like space in opened in a wall.

nitre: (n) a crystalline salt composed of potassium nitrate (KNO3) that grows in caves.

obstinate: (adj) not willing to follow along with popular opinion; stubborn.

palazzo: (n) Italian for palace or mansion.

promiscuously: (adv) without any thought or organization; random.

puncheon: (n) a large cask that can hold up to 454 liters of wine or liquid.

rampant: (adj) wild or violent.

rampart: (n) a pile.

rapier: (n) a sword with a long, narrow two-edged blade.

repose: (v) to lie dead.

rheum: (n) the watery mucous that comes from the eyes.

roquelaire: (n) now spelled roquelaure. A cloak that men wore in the 18th century. It clasped around the throat and extended to the knees.

sconce: (n) a bracket that held torches to the wall.

tier: (n) a row or level.

trowel: (n) a tool that masons use to apply mortar to bricks.

vault: (n) a large cellar or basement with arched walls and ceiling.

virtuoso: (adj) having great interest in the fine arts.

Study Questions

1. Does Poe ever create any sympathy for Fortunato, or are we supposed to be only appalled by Montresor's actions?

2. At the end of the story, Montresor calls Fortunato's name and gets no response. He even feels sickened. Does Montresor succeed in his revenge or is it only an empty gesture?

3. Does Montresor ever show signs of remorse? Or is he just a sociopath?

4. What is the symbolism of burying people alive? Poe uses this image in several other stories.

5. Is Montresor a reliable narrator? Can we believe everything he says in this story?

6. Does Fortunato ever show he is capable of insulting or hurting a person as Montresor says he has?

7. This story was very dark and horrifying at the time of its publication. Does the story horrify or disturb you in any way? Why or why not?

8. Poe was never considered a man of literary taste by his contemporaries. Does this story have any literary merit, or is it just a piece of "pulp fiction"? Explain your answer.

9. At first, we don't quite know what Montresor is going to do. At what point do we know about his intentions to murder? What are some of the clues?

II

THE ADVENTURES OF TOM SAWYER: CHAPTER 2

by Mark Twain (1867, The South: Missouri)

- Introduction of the Author
- Synopsis
- Text
- Words & Idioms
- Study Questions

Introduction of the Author: Mark Twain (1835-1910)

Samuel Clemens was born in Missouri and spent his early life near the grand Mississippi River that would have a great influence on his life and writing. He lived close to the frontier of the American West, where the Indian legends and the stories from black slaves influenced him the most. Missouri was a slave state, and Clemens often explored slavery in his works. Though owning slaves was legal in his state, he never supported it and often wrote against the immorality of it.

In 1857, Clemens worked as a river pilot on the Mississippi River, an occupation that was the most prestigious in the area and was a childhood dream of his. With the outbreak of the Civil War, the river boat business ended when the fighting disrupted trade. Clemens enlisted in the Confederate Army but decided it was not for him, so he moved further west to Nevada and then to California. Though he moved far from his home on the river, he kept to his roots, going so far as to adopt the pen name Mark Twain, which is a river pilot's term. It was shouted by a pilot to mean "all clear!" It actually means 3.6 meters of water, which is the depth needed for a boat to pass safely through.

While in the West, Twain mined for gold, but never struck it rich, except for an abundance of stories that he would turn into beloved novels. After the war, American interests started to move westward as realism mixed with humor was needed to

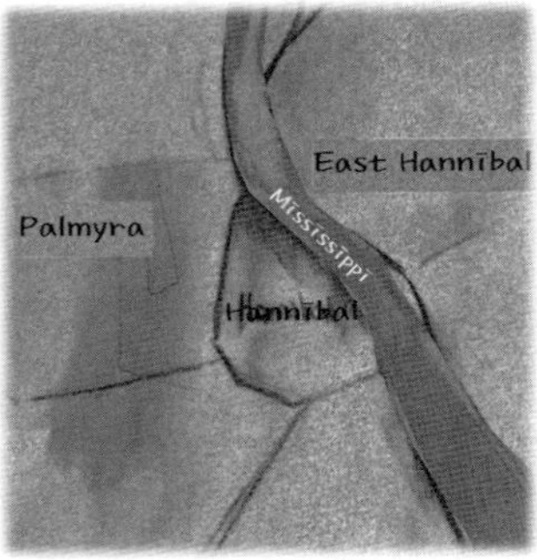

heal the broken spirit of the nation. Cowboys, Indians, train robbers, and gun fights were becoming part of a common genre called westerns. This free, purely American lifestyle was what set it apart from the those of the American East, whose writers wanted to write better than those in Europe. Never seeking to outperform European writers, Twain instead focused on all that was humorous in American life. He published his adventures out west in *Roughing It* (1872), a piece of semi-autobiographical travel literature. It features several tall tales—a buffalo climbs a tree to chase a hunter—and hoaxes. The hoax is an amusing tall tale common in the West and features a common person cheating and beating an expert. They were often written in newspapers, and many readers thought them to be true stories.

Perhaps Twain's most famous hoaxers are Tom Sawyer and Huck Finn. In *The Adventures of Tom Sawyer* (1876), Twain creates a loveable "bad boy" who is a rebel only because he fights against adult stupidity. Though he causes trouble, it is a righteous trouble, and in the end, he wins. Twain relies heavily on settings from his childhood home and geographical area to create a vividly rich novel. Tom is a romantic character, in that he always daydreams, loves reading of knights from the Middle Ages, and does everything with expectation for adventure. In the end, however, he is still a boy with a family who eventually grows up into manhood.

In contrast to Tom, Twain created Huck Finn in *The Adventures of Huckleberry Finn* (1884). Huck is also a troublemaker but more realistic than Tom. He is a homeless boy, whose life is harsh and anti-romantic. His adventures are not sought but are a part of his daily life. In the end, there are no family members to rescue him; he is truly an outsider. The novel is now rated as one of greatest works of American art, but it is still very controversial. It was criticized for its foul language, and several public libraries of his day would not allow it on their shelves. In modern times, it is criticized as racist, since it uses the derogatory word "nigger" rather freely. Many modern schools ban it from their reading lists for this reason.

Seventy-four years after he was born, Mark Twain passed away on April 21, 1910. In the company of his daughter and biographer, he died quietly in his sleep with a copy of Carlyle's *French Revolution* on the bed next to him.

Synopsis

It is a beautiful Saturday morning during summer vacation. Tom Sawyer shows up with a bucket of white paint and a paint brush. He is shocked to see how much fence he has to paint that day. He barely starts when he decides to take a break. He sees Jim, a local black kid, skipping past with a bucket of water that he is bringing from the town pump. Preferring to carry water over painting, Tom asks Jim to trade him chores.

Jim is afraid of getting into trouble if he switches chores, so Tom bribes him with a white marble. Jim almost accepts when he is chased away by Tom's Aunt, who asked Tom to paint the fence in the first place.

When Tom starts to think about other boys teasing him for having to work while they play, he gets more upset and comes up with a plan to get out of his chores. He gathers all his toys and other junk to exchange for work, but he knows it is not enough to buy any free time. However, he comes up with an alternate plan that will work better than bribery.

He sees Ben Rogers with a nice, juicy apple coming down the street, pretending to be a steam boat captain on an imaginary ship. Tom starts painting like it is the most interesting pleasure he has ever done, even more interesting than Ben's play.

When Tom continues his painting in earnest, Ben wants to give it a try. Tom refuses until Ben bribes him with the apple. Tom reluctantly allows Ben to paint. He then goes and sits in the shade munching on the apple while Ben sweats in the sun.

Later, more boys pass by to make fun, but Tom cons them into painting the fence as well. He continues this all afternoon. By evening, many boys have paid Tom their toys and trinkets to have a chance to paint the fence. He has to stop only because he has run out of paint.

Tom learns an important lesson about humanity. To make someone want a thing, you have to make the thing difficult to get. He also learns that the same activity can be either work or play. It is work if one is forced to do it like Tom was. It is fun if one has a chance to choose it like the boys did. This is the way of the world.

Text

Saturday morning was come, and all the summer world was bright and fresh, and brimming with life. There was a song in every heart; and if the heart was young the music issued at the lips. There was cheer in every face and a spring in every step. The locust-trees were in bloom and the fragrance of the blossoms filled the air. Cardiff Hill, beyond the village and above it, was green with vegetation and it lay just far enough away to seem a Delectable Land, dreamy, reposeful, and inviting.

Tom appeared on the sidewalk with a bucket of whitewash and a long-handled brush. He surveyed the fence, and all gladness left him and a deep melancholy settled down upon his spirit. Thirty yards of board fence nine feet high. Life to him seemed hollow, and existence but a burden. Sighing, he dipped his brush and passed it along the topmost plank; repeated the operation; did it again; compared the insignificant whitewashed streak with the far reaching continent of unwhitewashed fence, and sat down on a tree-box discouraged. Jim came skipping out at the gate with a tin pail, and singing Buffalo Gals. Bringing water from the town pump had always been hateful work in Tom's eyes, before, but now it did not strike him so. He remem-

bered that there was company at the pump. White, mulatto, and negro boys and girls were always there waiting their turns, resting, trading playthings, quarrelling, fighting, skylarking. And he remembered that although the pump was only a hundred and fifty yards off, Jim never got back with a bucket of water under an hour—and even then somebody generally had to go after him. Tom said:

"Say, Jim, I'll fetch the water if you'll whitewash some."

Jim shook his head and said:

"Can't, Mars Tom. Ole missis, she tole me I got to go an' git dis water an' not stop foolin'roun'wid anybody. She say she spec' Mars Tom gwine to ax me to whitewash, an' so she tole me go 'long an''tend to my own business—she 'lowed she'd 'tend to de whitewashin'."[1]

"Oh, never you mind what she said, Jim. That's the way she always talks. Gimme the bucket—I won't be gone only a a minute. She won't ever know."

"Oh, I dasn't, Mars Tom. Ole missis she'd take an' tar de head off'n me. 'Deed she would."[2]

"She! She never licks anybody—whacks 'em over the head with her thimble—and who cares for that, I'd like to know. She talks awful, but talk don't hurt—anyways it don't if she don't cry. Jim, I'll give you a marvel. I'll give you a white alley!"

Jim began to waver.

"White alley, Jim! And it's a bully taw."

"My! Dat's a mighty gay marvel, I tell you! But Mars Tom I's

1 Translation from the colloquial: Can't, Master Tom. Old Missus told me I have to go and get the water and not to stop to fool around with anybody. She expected Master Tom to ask me to whitewash, and she told me to go along and mind my own business. She said she would tend to the whitewashing.

2 Oh, I dare not to, Master Tom. Old Missus would take my entire head off of me. Indeed, she would.

powerful 'fraid ole missis—"[3]

"And besides, if you will I'll show you my sore toe."

Jim was only human—this attraction was too much for him. He put down his pail, took the white alley, and bent over the toe with absorbing interest while the bandage was being unwound. In another moment he was flying down the street with his pail and a tingling rear, Tom was whitewashing with vigor, and Aunt Polly was retiring from the field with a slipper in her hand and triumph in her eye.

But Tom's energy did not last. He began to think of the fun he had planned for this day, and his sorrows multiplied. Soon the free boys would come tripping along on all sorts of delicious expeditions, and they would make a world of fun of him for having to work—the very thought of it burnt him like fire. He got out his worldly wealth and examined it—bits of toys, marbles, and trash; enough to buy an exchange of work, maybe, but not half enough to buy so much as half an hour of pure freedom. So he returned his straitened means to his pocket, and gave up the idea of trying to buy the boys. At this dark and hopeless moment an inspiration burst upon him! Nothing less than a great, magnificent inspiration.

He took up his brush and went tranquilly to work. Ben Rogers hove in sight presently—the very boy, of all boys, whose ridicule he had been dreading. Ben's gait was the

3 Wow! That is a wonderfully bright toy, I tell you. But Master Tom, I'm really afraid of the Old Missus.

hop-skip-and-jump—proof enough that his heart was light and his anticipations high. He was eating an apple, and giving a long, melodious whoop, at intervals, followed by a deep-toned ding-dong-dong, ding-dong-dong, for he was personating a steamboat. As he drew near, he slackened speed, took the middle of the street, leaned far over to starboard and rounded to ponderously and with laborious pomp and circumstance—for he was personating the Big Missouri, and considered himself to be drawing nine feet of water. He was boat and captain and engine-bells combined, so he had to imagine himself standing on his own hurricane-deck giving the orders and executing them:

"Stop her, sir! Ting-a-ling-ling!" The headway ran almost out, and he drew up slowly toward the sidewalk.

"Ship up to back! Ting-a-ling-ling!" His arms straightened and stiffened down his sides.

"Set her back on the stabboard! Ting-a-ling-ling! Chow! ch-chow-wow! Chow!"His right hand, mean-time, describing stately circles—for it was representing a forty-foot wheel.

"Let her go back on the labboard! Ting-a-ling-ling! Chow-ch-chow-chow!" The left hand began to describe circles.

"Stop the stabboard! Ting-a-ling-ling! Stop the labboard! Come ahead on the stabboard! Stop her! Let your outside turn over slow! Ting-a-ling-ling! Chow-ow-ow! Get out that head-line! lively now! Come—out with your spring-line —what're you about there! Take a turn round that stump with the bight of it! Stand by that stage, now—let her go! Done with the engines, sir! Ting-a-ling-ling! SH'T! S'H'T! SH'T!" (trying the gauge-cocks).

Tom went on whitewashing—paid no attention to the steamboat. Ben stared a moment and then said: "Hi-Yi! You're up a stump, ain't you!"

No answer. Tom surveyed his last touch with the eye of an artist, then he gave his brush another gentle sweep and surveyed the result, as before. Ben ranged up alongside of him. Tom's mouth watered for the apple, but he stuck to his work. Ben said:

"Hello, old chap, you got to work, hey?"

Tom wheeled suddenly and said:

"Why, it's you, Ben! I warn't noticing."

"Say—I'm going in a-swimming, I am. Don't you wish you could? But of course you'd druther work—wouldn't you? Course you would!"

Tom contemplated the boy a bit, and said:

"What do you call work?"

"Why, ain't that work?"

Tom resumed his whitewashing, and answered carelessly:

"Well, maybe it is, and maybe it ain't. All I know, is, it suits Tom Sawyer."

"Oh come, now, you don't mean to let on that you like it?"

The brush continued to move.

"Like it? Well, I don't see why I oughtn't to like it. Does a boy get a chance to whitewash a fence every day?"

That put the thing in a new light. Ben stopped nibbling his apple. Tom swept his brush daintily back and forth—stepped back to note the effect—added a touch here and there—criticised the effect again—Ben watching every move and getting more and more interested, more and more absorbed. Presently he said:

"Say, Tom, let me whitewash a little."

Tom considered, was about to consent; but he altered his mind:

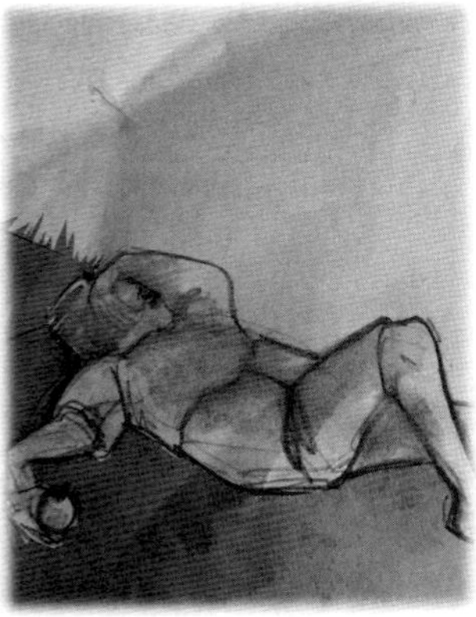

"No—no—I reckon it wouldn't hardly do, Ben. You see, Aunt Polly's awful particular about this fence—right here on the street, you know—but if it was the back fence I wouldn't mind and she wouldn't. Yes, she's awful particular about this fence; it's got to be done very careful; I reckon there ain't one boy in a thousand, maybe two thousand, that can do it the way it's got to be done."

"No—is that so? Oh come, now—lemme just try. Only just a little—I'd let you, if you was me, Tom."

"Ben, I'd like to, honest injun; but Aunt Polly—well, Jim wanted to do it, but she wouldn't let him; Sid wanted to do it, and she wouldn't let Sid. Now don't you see how I'm fixed? If you was to tackle this fence and anything was to happen to it—"

"Oh, shucks, I'll be just as careful. Now lemme try. Say—I'll give you the core of my apple."

"Well, here—No, Ben, now don't. I'm afeard—"

"I'll give you all of it!"

Tom gave up the brush with reluctance in his face, but alacrity in his heart. And while the late steamer Big Missouri worked and sweated in the sun, the retired artist sat on a barrel in the shade close by, dangled his legs, munched his apple, and planned the slaughter of more innocents. There was no lack of material; boys happened along every little while; they came to jeer, but remained to whitewash. By the time Ben was fagged out, Tom had traded the next chance to Billy Fisher for a kite, in good repair; and when he played out, Johnny Miller bought in for a dead rat and a string to swing it with—and so on, and so on, hour after hour. And when the middle of the afternoon came, from being a poor poverty-stricken boy in the morning, Tom was literally rolling in wealth. He had besides the things before mentioned, twelve marbles, part of a jews-harp, a piece of blue bottle-glass to look through, a spool cannon, a key that wouldn't unlock anything, a fragment of chalk, a glass stopper of a decanter, a tin soldier, a couple of tadpoles, six fire-crackers, a kitten with only one eye, a brass door-knob, a dog-collar—but no dog—the handle of a knife, four pieces of orange peel, and a dilapidated old window sash.

He had had a nice, good, idle time all the while—plenty of company—and the fence had three coats of whitewash on it! If he hadn't run out of whitewash he would have bankrupted every boy in the village.

Tom said to himself that it was not such a hollow world, after all. He had discovered a great law of human action, without knowing it—namely, that in order to make a man or a boy covet a thing, it is only necessary to make the thing difficult to attain. If he had been a great and wise philosopher, like the writer of this book, he would now have comprehended that Work consists of whatever a body is obliged to do, and that Play consists of whatever a body is not obliged to do. And this would help him to understand why constructing artificial flowers or performing on a tread-mill is work, while rolling ten-pins or climbing Mont Blanc is only amusement. There are wealthy gentlemen in England who drive four-horse passenger-coaches twenty or thirty miles on a daily line,

in the summer, because the privilege costs them considerable money; but if they were offered wages for the service, that would turn it into work and then they would resign.

The boy mused awhile over the substantial change which had taken place in his worldly circumstances, and then wended toward headquarters to report.

Words & Idioms

ain't: (slang) colloquial slang meaning "am not".
alacrity: (n) joyful willingness
afeard: (adj) afraid
Big Missouri: (n) the name of a steam boat
bully taw: (n) a marble that is considered better than other marbles
decanter: (n) a decorative glass bottle for serving wine or alcohol
delectable: (adj) delightful or pleasing
dilapidated: (adj) run down or damaged beyond repair
fagged out: (v) to be tired after working; exhausted
gauge-cock: (n) a type of instrument for measuring steam on a steam boat.
gay: (adj) older use meaning a bright and eye-catching
honest injun: (idiom) "I'm telling the truth." Injun is a colloquial (and offensive) form of Indian.
issue: (v) to pass or flow out of something
labboard: (n) mispronunciation of "larboard," the left-hand side of a water or air vessel
lemme: (v phr) colloquial for "let me"
lick: (v) informal use meaning hit or beat
marvel: (n) a thing that gives wonder
Mars Tom: (slang) Master Tom
melancholy: (n) sadness
Mont Blank: (n) the highest mountain in the Alps
mulatto: (n) an older (and offensive) use meaning a person with both black and white ancestors
personate: (v) impersonate; to act like a person or thing

reposeful: (adj) calm and quiet
skylark: (v) to run around, free like a bird
slacken: (v) to decrease
spool cannon: (n phr) a homemade slingshot made from an elastic band and spool that can shoot a pencil
stabboard: (n) mispronunciation of "starboard"
starboard: (n) the right-hand side of a water or air vessel
straitened means: (n phr) poor; without money
wend: (v) go; walk
white alley: a type of white marble that is used specifically for shooting at other marbles
whitewash: (n) a type of white colored paint

Study Questions

1. What do you think of Tom Sawyer as a protagonist? Is he a sympathetic protagonist? Explain your answer.

2. What important lesson does Tom learn at the end of the chapter?

3. The moral of the story is given at the end of the chapter. What does Tom learn about life? Is this still true today? Give some examples from your life and times where this is true.

4. The world of Tom Sawyer is a microcosm of adulthood. What do we learn about the Mark Twain's world from this story? Hint: steamboats, black slave boys, and rough boys.

5. Based on this chapter alone, is Tom just a troublemaker? Is there evidence of his role in his youth centered society?

6. How mature does Tom appear to be? Is this a realistic depiction of a young boy? Explain your answer.

7. How does Tom's plan to get Jim to paint the fence compare with his plan to get Ben to do it? Why was he successful the second time and not the first time?

8. Some readers argue that Tom has an instinctive understanding of human character. What human characteristic is revealed in this chapter?

9. If work is doing what you have to do and play is doing what you want to do, then is it possible to never work your whole life? Explain your answer.

III

THE STORY OF AN HOUR

by Kate Chopin (1894, The South: Louisiana)

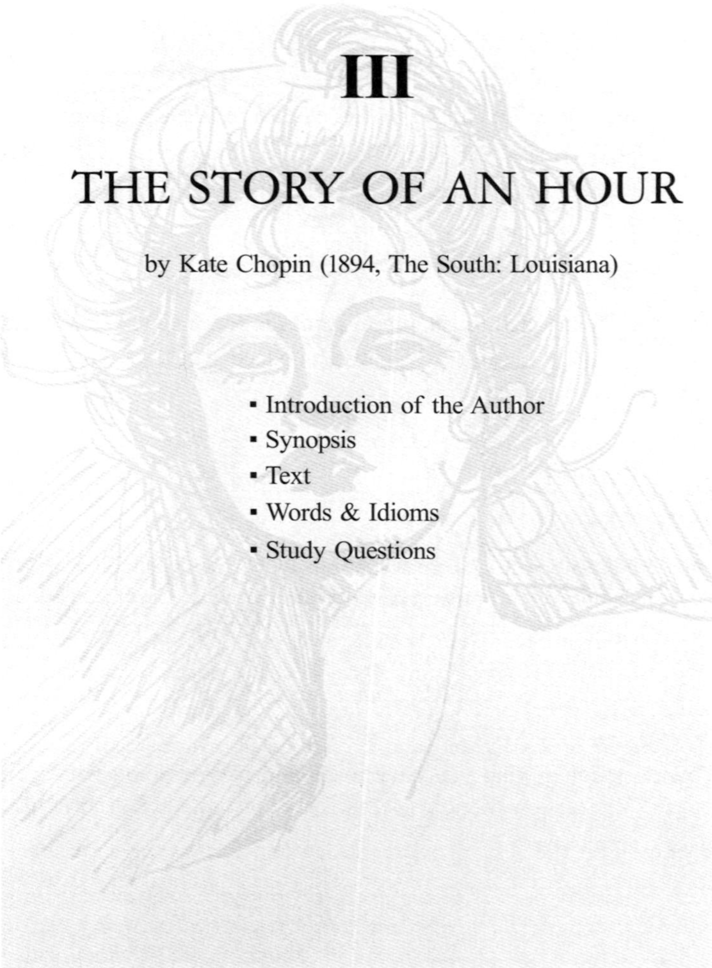

- Introduction of the Author
- Synopsis
- Text
- Words & Idioms
- Study Questions

Introduction of the Author: Kate Chopin (1850-1904)

Catherine O'Flaherty was born on July 12, 1850 in St. Louis, Missouri, the youngest of three to an immigrant Irishman, Thomas O'Flaherty and a French-American mother, Eliza Faris. With the death of her father in 1855, Kate found herself living with a widowed mother, grandmother, and great-grandmother, all who were smart, independent women. That same year, she entered the Sacred Heart Academy, a Catholic boarding school known for highly intelligent nuns, where she found a love for books, especially the writings of Sir Walter Scott and Charles Dickens. By the time she was thirteen, she had decided to drop out of traditional school entirely and devote her education to books. Such independence lasted only two years when she decided to return to Sacred Heart Academy. She graduated at the top of her class with a penchant for superb story telling.

In 1870, she married Oscar Chopin, who was a fair man of liberal thinking and afforded his new wife all the luxuries and freedom an intelligent, independent woman could want. She was even known to walk through the city streets unaccompanied by her husband, which caused quite a stir amongst the locals. Oscar bought a cotton plantation, which he didn't manage very effectively. By the time she was 28, she had given birth to five boys and two girls. Four years later, Oscar died of swamp fever, leaving his widow and seven kids in considerable debt. Selling the plantation, Kate moved in with her mother, only to see her die the next year.

Forced to alternative means of making money, Kate turned to writing, where she set her pen to the lifestyle and

people she knew in Louisiana. She published her first novel, *At Fault*, in 1890 but had already started her writing career the previous year with the publication of three short stories. "The Story of an Hour," perhaps her most anthologized short story, was published in 1891. The focus of independent women in these stories shut editors off from her work, and she was forced to pay for the publication of her first novel.

Her highest critical acclaim came in 1894 with the publication of a collection of short stories in *Bayou Folk,* which showcased the classical Chopin characters of self-reliant women struggling for purpose in a male dominated society. She followed the success of her first collection with a second in 1897, *A Night in Acadia.*

However, it is with her most respected novel to date that nearly ruined her profession. *The Awakening*, published in 1899, marked the turning point of her literary career by proving that she was a novelist worthy of remembrance;

critics may consider it an American masterpiece now, but it ended her critical reputation and vocation as a writer. America at the time was not yet ready for the strong feminist viewpoint of Chopin or her novel's protagonist, Edna Pontellier, who "awakens" into the full independence and sexuality of womanhood that is applauded by readers today. The critical backlash surprised Chopin, which hurt her deeply, causing her to destroy the manuscript, and over the next five years, she only published a couple of short stories that readers mostly ignored.

Five years after her dismal failure, Kate Chopin died, forgotten and resentful, from a brain hemorrhage in 1904. Though her critics had managed to destroy her literary life, and her contemporary fans had abandoned her, Chopin' s writings found renewed interest in the 1960's, and she became the leading feminist voice of her time.

Synopsis

Mrs. Mallard, a typical Victorian woman, oppressed and emotionally tied to her husband, is suffering from a heart condition. Upon learning that her husband has died in a train crash, Mrs. Mallard confines herself to her room to properly mourn the passing of her husband. Upon deeper contemplation, she soon starts to see that her life isn't over now that her husband has passed, but is, in fact, just beginning. She is now free. Finding the strength and the will to continue as an "independent" woman, Ms. Mallard now emerges from the isolation of her room.

Upon her descent down the stairs, she notices someone entering the house. It is none other than Mr. Mallard; the sight of which causes the heart of poor Mrs. Mallard to stop, killing her. Though all who witness this unfortunate event conclude that Mrs. Mallard has died from the joy of her husband's return, the reader sees the irony of his return; she dies not from joy, but from the shock of losing her new -found life.

Text

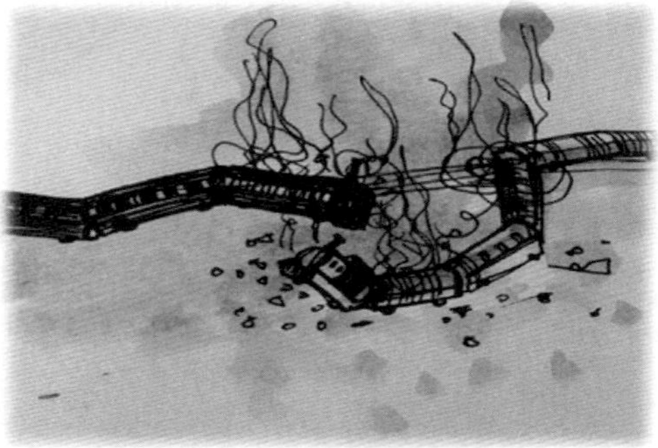

Knowing that Mrs. Mallard was afflicted with a heart trouble, great care was taken to break to her as gently as possible the news of her husband's death.

It was her sister Josephine who told her, in broken sentences; veiled hints that revealed in half concealing. Her husband's friend Richards was there, too, near her. It was he who had been in the newspaper office when intelligence of the railroad disaster was received, with Brently Mallard's name leading the list of "killed." He had only taken the time to assure himself of its truth by a second telegram, and had hastened to forestall any less careful, less tender friend in bearing the sad message.

She did not hear the story as many women have heard the same, with a paralyzed inability to accept its significance. She wept at once, with sudden, wild abandonment, in her sister's arms. When the storm of grief had spent itself she went away to her room alone. She would have no one follow her.

There stood, facing the open window, a comfortable, roomy armchair. Into this she sank, pressed down by a physical exhaustion that haunted her body and seemed to reach into her soul.

She could see in the open square before her house the tops of trees that were all aquiver with the new spring life.

The delicious breath of rain was in the air. In the street below a peddler was crying his wares. The notes of a distant song which some one was singing reached her faintly, and countless sparrows were twittering in the eaves.

There were patches of blue sky showing here and there through the clouds that had met and piled one above the other in the west facing her window.

She sat with her head thrown back upon the cushion of the chair, quite motionless, except when a sob came up into her throat and shook her, as a child who has cried itself to sleep continues to sob in its dreams.

She was young, with a fair, calm face, whose lines bespoke repression and even a certain strength. But now there was a dull stare in her eyes, whose gaze was fixed away off yonder on one of those patches of blue sky. It was not a glance of reflection, but rather indicated a suspension of intelligent thought.

There was something coming to her and she was waiting for it, fearfully. What was it? She did not know; it was too subtle and elusive to name. But she felt it, creeping out of the sky, reaching toward her through the sounds, the scents, the color that filled the air.

Now her bosom rose and fell tumultuously. She was beginning to recognize this thing that was approaching to possess her, and she was striving to beat it back with her will--as powerless as her two white slender hands would have been.

When she abandoned herself a little whispered word escaped her slightly parted lips. She said it over and over under her breath: "free, free, free!" The vacant stare and the look of terror that had followed it went from her eyes. They stayed keen and bright. Her pulses beat fast, and the coursing blood warmed and relaxed every inch of her body.

She did not stop to ask if it were or were not a monstrous joy that held her. A clear and exalted perception enabled her to dismiss the suggestion as trivial.

She knew that she would weep again when she saw the kind, tender hands folded in death; the face that had never looked save with love upon her, fixed and gray and dead. But she saw beyond that bitter moment a long procession of years to come that would belong to her absolutely. And she opened and spread her arms out to them in welcome.

There would be no one to live for during those coming years; she would live for herself. There would be no powerful will bending hers in that blind persistence with which men and women believe they have a right to impose a private will upon a fellow-creature. A kind intention or a cruel intention made the act seem no less a crime as she looked upon it in that brief moment of illumination.

And yet she had loved him--sometimes. Often she had not. What did it matter! What could love, the unsolved mystery, count for in face of this possession of self-assertion which she suddenly recognized as the strongest impulse of her being!

"Free! Body and soul free!" she kept whispering.

Josephine was kneeling before the closed door with her lips to the keyhole, imploring for admission. "Louise, open the door! I beg, open the door--you will make yourself ill. What are you doing Louise? For heaven's sake open the door."

"Go away. I am not making myself ill." No; she was drinking in a very elixir of life through that open window.

Her fancy was running riot along those days ahead of her. Spring days, and summer days, and all sorts of days that would be her own. She breathed a quick prayer that life might be long. It was only yesterday she had thought with a shudder that life might be long.

She arose at length and opened the door to her sister's importunities. There was a feverish triumph in her eyes, and she carried herself unwittingly like a goddess of Victory. She clasped her sister's waist, and together they descended the stairs. Richards stood waiting for them at the bottom.

Some one was opening the front door with a latchkey. It was Brently Mallard who entered, a little travel-stained, composedly carrying his grip-sack and umbrella. He had been far from the scene of accident, and did not even know there had been one. He stood amazed at Josephine's piercing cry; at Richards' quick motion to screen him from the view of his wife.

But Richards was too late.

When the doctors came they said she had died of heart disease-- of joy that kills.

Words & Idioms

afflicted: (adj) troubled with physical suffering, especially a disease.
aquiver: (adj) shaking or trembling.
bespeak: (v) to show or indicate.
course: (v) to move quickly or pump.
elixir: (n) a medicinal cure for all ills.
forestall: (v) to delay.
grip-sack: (n) a small travel case.
importunity: (n) a constant, nagging request.
impose: (v) to force.
keen: (adj) sharp and bright.
repression: (n) the state of controlling something by force.
self-assertion: (n) positive development of one's own behavior.
subtle: (adj) small or difficult to comprehend.
telegram: (n) a message received by a telegraph (the sending and receiving of electrical signals by wire), often before the invention of the telephone.
tumultuously: (adv) in a violent or forced manner.
twittering: (v) the chirping sound a bird makes; chirruping.
veiled: (adj) hidden.

Study Questions

1. The first thing that we read about Mrs. Mallard is that she has heart trouble, and other people respond to her according to this condition. How might heart trouble be more than a physical illness? Evidently, this seems to be an important part of who she is. So who do you think took care to break her the news of her husband's death?

2. Why is this story written in the passive voice, with a hidden narrator? Why is there a secondary narrator? Was the narrator present at the time of this incident or is the narrator telling a second-hand tale?

3. What are the clues in the story that Mrs. Mallard's physical and mental conditions are connected? How does this clue us into what will happen at the end of the story?

4. Look for repeated uses of the negatives and positives in the story. What are some examples of these? Why are positives and negatives used in this way? What is the purpose they play in this story?

5. The story is short, but we get rich details as to what kind of woman Mrs. Mallard is. What sort of person is she? Is this a positive or a negative portrayal of her? Give examples to support your answer.

6. What is Mrs. Mallard's, or possibly Kate Chopin's, general view of relationships between men and women? Do you agree with this view? Why or why not?

7. We get only a brief but accurate description of the husband: "It was Brently Mallard who entered, a little **travel-stained,** composedly carrying his **grip-sack** and umbrella." If he was not on the train, then why is he stained by travel? This is our main picture of him; does it go beyond the state of his clothing? It is a "grip-sack," not a "briefcase" or "suitcase"; what does this word suggest (again, given that we have been told almost nothing else about him)? Does his distance echo, in figurative terms, the nature of their marriage?

8. Mrs. Mallard dies from "the joy that kills." Whose interests does this diagnosis serve? How is it reflective of Chopin's implied view of marriage?

IV

THE GIFT OF THE MAGI

by O. Henry (1903, The South: Texas)

- Introduction of the Author
- Synopsis
- Text
- Words & Idioms
- Study Questions

Introduction of the Author: O. Henry (1862-1910)

William Sydney Porter, better known by his pen name O. Henry, lived a life as exciting as the fiction he wrote. He was born in Greensboro, North Carolina where his great uncle served as governor. After his mother died of tuberculosis when he was three, he and his father moved in with his grandmother. He later lived with his aunt and attended her elementary school. Though he loved to read, and his aunt continued to tutor him, he quit school at the age of fifteen. He started working as a clerk in his uncle's pharmacy and then received an apprenticeship as a pharmacist.

At the age of twenty, Porter moved to southern Texas to alleviate a chronic cough condition he had contracted. He worked on a sheep ranch for two years and eloped with Athol Estes, a seventeen-year-old who also had tuberculosis. His son died at birth, and he had a daughter a year later. His health improved, so he moved to Austin, Texas where he found work as a clerk in a real-estate office. He also worked as a pharmacist, draftsman, and a bank teller for the First National Bank. Interestingly, though the pastoral life had cured his illnesses, he became an alcoholic due to the the stress and demands of urban living. His drinking 2.3 liters of whiskey a day had a detrimental effect on his health later in life.

Porter moved to Houston, Texas in 1896 to write columns for the Post. A year later, the First National Bank was audited, and Porter's poor bookkeeping got him in trouble. He was arrested for embezzlement, a crime he denied committing and was transferred back to Austin to stand trial.

After his father-in-law bailed him out of jail, he fled to New Orleans, Louisiana and then to Honduras, Central America. Since his wife was sick and dying, she could not meet him in Central America, so he returned to the U.S. to face the courts. Athol soon died from tuberculosis. A little less than a year later, Porter was also found guilty of embezzlement and sentenced to five years in the Ohio penitentiary in 1898 but was released after three years for good behavior.

Though Porter had written several stories before his imprisonment, he penned fourteen short stories while incarcerated, all under various pen names, to help support his daughter. After his release from prison, he changed his name to O. Henry. Many speculations arise as to why he settled on such a name. One is from Porter himself, who said he chose "Henry" randomly from a newspaper and then settled on an easy initial to write, "O." He gave more reasons in other interviews, causing readers to speculate on the origins as well. American writers and intellectuals even surmised that the name O. Henry originated from the name of his prison, **Oh**io **Pen**itentiar**y**. Other speculators say that the name came from the prison warden Orren Henry.

In 1902, Porter moved to New York, where many of his stories take place, to fully concentrate on his writing. One of his last anthology collections *The Four Million* (1906) expressed his appreciations for his readers, especially the people of New York—New York had a population of four million at the time of publication. Most noteworthy of this publication was the short story "The Gift of the Magi," which next to Charles Dickens's "A Christmas Carol," is the most adapted short story.

Porter became a prolific writer and wrote a story a week over a three-year period. During the last eight years of his life, he published 381 stories under the O. Henry pseud-

onym. Most of his stories were collected in anthologies (ten in all), and his total stories written stands at over 600. Not every story he wrote was a classic, but his ironic wit and twist endings endeared him to a wide following of readers, while most literary critics ignored him. Having such an extensive experience from living in both rural and urban settings, visiting foreign countries, and spending time in jail, Porter drew upon these to depict all the different aspects of American life and perspectives. Most of his stories are masterly crafted; just about any short story anthology includes an O. Henry story. Thus, he has become one of the most popular American writers.

Porter's heavy drinking had so affected his health that by 1908 his condition had worsened, interfering with his ability to write. On June 5, 1910, William Sydney Porter died from a liver disease and an enlarged heart.

Synopsis

It is the day before, Christmas, and Della has little money to buy her husband Jim a present. Even after saving pennies and shopping frugally for months, she only has $1.87 for shopping. She wishes to buy him a worthy gift, but her current amount can do no such thing.

The only items considered valuable by both Della and Jim are his gold watch, an heirloom handed down to him from his father, and her beautiful hair. These are the two possessions both find to be worth more than the jewels and treasures of royalty. Though she wears shabby and dull clothes, Della's hair makes up for that and adds radiance to her looks.

Thus, on Christmas Eve, Della makes up her mind. She enters a hair salon to sell her luxurious hair for twenty dollars.

Feeling satisfied, Della heads to the stores to find the perfect gift for Jim. After hours of searching, she finally comes across a chain for Jim's precious pocket. It is the only gift worthy of Jim and his heirloom. It costs exactly twenty-one dollars, and she even takes home 87 cents change, which is still a fair amount of money back then.

When she reaches home, she realizes how short her hair is and attempts to make her hair curly and presentable for her husband. After 40 minutes of curling her hair, the only result she can see is that she now looks like a school boy. She fears Jim's disappointment. He loved her hair so much. She worries but feels she has chosen wisely because of the gift she can buy him.

She prepares a dinner and waits with her gift in hand for Jim to return home from work. Her anxiety over her looks increases, and she says a little prayer that her husband will still find her beautiful.

Upon his entrance, he sees her and has an expression on his face that Della had not anticipated. She is not sure how he feels upon seeing her. Perhaps disappointment.

She runs to him, begging him not to feel bad, and that she had cut her hair for a gift. After all, hair grows back quickly.

Jim is dumbfounded. All he can do is repeat that she has cut her hair. She thinks he is disappointed and keeps reiterating that she did it all for him.

Jim finally comes out of his stupor long enough to hug her. He then pulls a gift from his coat pocket and tosses it on the table. He explains that nothing she does with her hair would make him love her any less. It is only his gift that has caused him so much grief.

Della opens the gift in anticipation, only to fall into a fit of tears soon after. In the package sit two combs she has always wanted, combs that would have ornamented her beautiful, luxurious hair if she had any left. Still, her hair will grow back, and she thanks Jim for the most precious gift.

Della leaps to her feet and excitedly offers her gift to Jim. She even offers to put the chain on his watch. Upon seeing the watch chain, he collapses onto the sofa, dumbfounded.

He sold his watch to buy her the gift of combs!

Text

One dollar and eighty-seven cents. That was all. And sixty cents of it was in pennies. Pennies saved one and two at a time by bulldozing the grocer and the vegetable man and the butcher until one's cheeks burned with the silent imputation of parsimony that such close dealing implied. Three times Della counted it. One dollar and eighty-seven cents. And the next day would be Christmas.

There was clearly nothing to do but flop down on the shabby little couch and howl. So Della did it. Which instigates the moral reflection that life is made up of sobs, sniffles, and smiles, with sniffles predominating.

While the mistress of the home is gradually subsiding from the first stage to the second, take a look at the home. A furnished flat at $8 per week. It did not exactly beggar description, but it certainly had that word on the lookout for the mendicancy squad.

In the vestibule below was a letter-box into which no letter would go, and an electric button from which no mortal finger could coax a ring. Also appertaining thereunto was a card bearing the name "Mr. James Dillingham Young."

The "Dillingham" had been flung to the breeze during a former period of prosperity when its possessor was being paid $30 per week. Now, when the income was shrunk to $20, though, they were thinking seriously of contracting to a modest and unassuming D. But whenever Mr. James Dillingham Young came home and reached his flat above he was called "Jim" and greatly hugged by Mrs. James Dillingham Young, already introduced to you as Della. Which is all very good.

Della finished her cry and attended to her cheeks with

the powder rag. She stood by the window and looked out dully at a gray cat walking a gray fence in a gray backyard. Tomorrow would be Christmas Day, and she had only $1.87 with which to buy Jim a present. She had been saving every penny she could for months, with this result. Twenty dollars a week doesn't go far. Expenses had been greater than she had calculated. They always are. Only $1.87 to buy a present for Jim. Her Jim. Many a happy hour she had spent planning for something nice for him. Something fine and rare and sterling—something just a little bit near to being worthy of the honor of being owned by Jim.

There was a pier-glass between the windows of the room. Perhaps you have seen a pier-glass in an $8 flat. A very thin and very agile person may, by observing his reflection in a rapid sequence of longitudinal strips, obtain a fairly accurate conception of his looks. Della, being slender, had mastered the art.

Suddenly she whirled from the window and stood before the glass. Her eyes were shining brilliantly, but her face had lost its color within twenty seconds. Rapidly she pulled down her hair and let it fall to its full length.

Now, there were two possessions of the James Dillingham Youngs in which they both took a mighty pride. One was Jim's gold watch that had been his father's and his grandfather's. The other was Della's hair. Had the queen of Sheba lived in the flat across the airshaft, Della would have let her hair hang out the window some day to dry just to depreciate Her Majesty's jewels and gifts. Had King Solomon been the janitor, with all his treasures piled up in the basement, Jim would have pulled out his watch every time he passed, just to see him pluck at his beard from envy.

So now Della's beautiful hair fell about her rippling and shining like a cascade of brown waters. It reached below her

knee and made itself almost a garment for her. And then she did it up again nervously and quickly. Once she faltered for a minute and stood still while a tear or two splashed on the worn red carpet.

On went her old brown jacket; on went her old brown hat. With a whirl of skirts and with the brilliant sparkle still in her eyes, she fluttered out the door and down the stairs to the street.

Where she stopped the sign read: "Mne. Sofronie. Hair Goods of All Kinds." One flight up Della ran, and collected herself, panting. Madame, large, too white, chilly, hardly looked the "Sofronie."

"Will you buy my hair?" asked Della.

"I buy hair," said Madame. "Take yer hat off and let's have a sight at the looks of it."

Down rippled the brown cascade.

"Twenty dollars," said Madame, lifting the mass with a practiced hand.

"Give it to me quick," said Della.

Oh, and the next two hours tripped by on rosy wings. Forget the hashed metaphor. She was ransacking the stores for Jim's present.

She found it at last. It surely had been made for Jim and no one else. There was no other like it in any of the stores, and she had turned all of them inside out. It was a platinum fob chain simple and chaste in design, properly proclaiming its value by substance alone and not by meretricious ornamentation—as all good things should do. It was even worthy of The Watch. As soon as she saw it she knew that it must be Jim's. It was like him. Quietness and value—the de-

scription applied to both. Twenty-one dollars they took from her for it, and she hurried home with the 87 cents. With that chain on his watch Jim might be properly anxious about the time in any company. Grand as the watch was, he sometimes looked at it on the sly on account of the old leather strap that he used in place of a chain.

When Della reached home her intoxication gave way a little to prudence and reason. She got out her curling irons and lighted the gas and went to work repairing the ravages made by generosity added to love. Which is always a tremendous task, dear friends—a mammoth task.

Within forty minutes her head was covered with tiny, close-lying curls that made her look wonderfully like a truant schoolboy. She looked at her reflection in the mirror long, carefully, and critically.

"If Jim doesn't kill me," she said to herself, "before he takes a second look at me, he'll say I look like a Coney Island chorus girl. But what could I do—oh! what could I do with a dollar and eighty seven cents?"

At 7 o'clock the coffee was made and the frying-pan was on the back of the stove hot and ready to cook the chops.

Jim was never late. Della doubled the fob chain in her hand and sat on the corner of the table near the door that he always entered. Then she heard his step on the stair away down on the first flight, and she turned white for just a moment. She had a habit for saying little silent prayer about the simplest everyday things, and now she whispered: "Please God, make him think I am still pretty."

The door opened and Jim stepped in and closed it. He looked thin and very serious. Poor fellow, he was only twenty-two—and to be burdened with a family! He needed a new overcoat and he was without gloves.

Jim stopped inside the door, as immovable as a setter at the scent of quail. His eyes were fixed upon Della, and there was an expression in them that she could not read, and it terrified her. It was not anger, nor surprise, nor disapproval, nor horror, nor any of the sentiments that she had been prepared for. He simply stared at her fixedly with that peculiar expression on his face.

Della wriggled off the table and went for him.

"Jim, darling," she cried, "don't look at me that way. I had my hair cut off and sold because I couldn't have lived through Christmas without giving you a present. It'll grow out again—you won't mind, will you? I just had to do it. My hair grows awfully fast. Say 'Merry Christmas!' Jim, and let' s be happy. You don't know what a nice—what a beautiful, nice gift I've got for you."

"You've cut off your hair?" asked Jim, laboriously, as if he had not arrived at that patent fact yet even after the hardest mental labor.

"Cut it off and sold it," said Della. "Don't you like me just as well, anyhow? I'm me without my hair, ain't I?"

Jim looked about the room curiously.

"You say your hair is gone?" he said, with an air almost of idiocy.

"You needn't look for it," said Della. "It's sold, I tell you—sold and gone, too. It's Christmas Eve, boy. Be good to me, for it went for you. Maybe the hairs of my head were numbered," she went on with sudden serious sweetness, "but nobody could ever count my love for you. Shall I put the chops on, Jim?"

Out of his trance Jim seemed quickly to wake. He enfolded his Della. For ten seconds let us regard with discreet scrutiny some inconsequential object in the other direction. Eight dollars a week or a million a year—what is the difference? A mathematician or a wit would give you the wrong answer. The magi brought valuable gifts, but that was not among them. This dark assertion will be illuminated later on.

Jim drew a package from his overcoat pocket and threw it upon the table.

"Don't make any mistake, Dell," he said, "about me. I don't think there's anything in the way of a haircut or a shave or a shampoo that could make me like my girl any less. But if you'll unwrap that package you may see why you had me going a while at first."

White fingers and nimble tore at the string and paper. And then an ecstatic scream of joy; and then, alas! a quick feminine change to hysterical tears and wails, necessitating the immediate employment of all the comforting powers of the lord of the flat.

For there lay The Combs—the set of combs, side and back, that Della had worshipped long in a Broadway window. Beautiful combs, pure tortoise shell, with jeweled rims—just the shade to wear in the beautiful vanished hair. They were expensive combs, she knew, and her heart had simply craved and yearned over them without the least hope of possession. And now, they were hers, but the tresses that should have adorned the coveted adornments were gone.

But she hugged them to her bosom,

and at length she was able to look up with dim eyes and a smile and say: "My hair grows so fast, Jim!"

And then Della leaped up like a little singed cat and cried, "Oh, oh!"

Jim had not yet seen his beautiful present. She held it out to him eagerly upon her open palm. The dull precious metal seemed to flash with a reflection of her bright and ardent spirit.

"Isn't it a dandy, Jim? I hunted all over town to find it. You'll have to look at the time a hundred times a day now. Give me your watch. I want to see how it looks on it."

Instead of obeying, Jim tumbled down on the couch and put his hands under the back of his head and smiled.

"Dell," said he, "let's put our Christmas presents away and keep 'em a while. They're too nice to use just at present. I sold the watch to get the money to your combs. And now suppose you put the chops on."

The magi, as you know, were wise men—wonderfully wise men—who brought gifts to the Babe in the manger. They invented the art of giving Christmas presents. Being wise, their gifts were no doubt wise ones, possibly bearing the privilege of exchange in case of duplication. And here I have lamely related to you the uneventful chronicle of two foolish children in a flat who most unwisely sacrificed for each other the greatest treasures of their house. But in a last word to the wise of these days let it be said that of all who give gifts these two were the wisest. Of all who give and receive gifts, such as they are wisest. Everywhere they are wisest. They are the magi.

Words & Idioms

$1.87: inflation adjusted to be about $41.00 (please note the inflation conversion is to give a sense of how much said amount would be in today's American market. It does not indicate exact value or buying power)
$20: inflation adjusted to about $443.00
$30: inflation adjusted to about $664.00
$8: inflation adjusted to about $177.00
60 cents: inflation adjusted to be about $14.00 (similar to saying that 14 dollars was in single bills.)
'em: colloquial for "them"
ardent: (adj) passionate
beggar description...mendicancy squad: a play on words where "beggar" here means inadequate but beggars (mendicancy squad) would feel at home living in it. This seems to say that the value they had to pay did not equal the run-down state of the apartment.
Broadway: (n) a wide avenue in Manhattan, New York; famous for theaters
flat: (n) apartment
fob chain: (n. phr) a chain that is attached to a pocket watch and then secured to a fob (the small pocket attached to the inside front pocket on a pair of pants)
hashed: (adj) messy
imputation of parsimony: (n. phr.) accusing someone of being stingy
King Solomon: legendary ruler of Israel mentioned in the Bible; famous for his wealth and wisdom

Magi: (n) in the Bible, the three wise men who brought the infant Jesus expensive gifts as homage
mendicancy squad: (n. phr.) beggars
meretricious: (adj) flashy; overly ornamental
pier-glass: (n. phr) a long mirror through which you view your whole body
Queen of Sheba: legendary queen mentioned in the Bible who ruled an area now in modern Ethiopia; famous for bestowing Solomon with caravans of riches after he solved her riddle
sterling (n): fine silver
tress: (n) locks of curly hair
yer: (pron) colloquial for "your"

Study Questions

1. The power of three is a potent symbol in this story. For example, there are three gifts of the Magi, three gifts of the Youngs (gold chain, comb, and love), three characters Jim, Della, and Madame Sofronie), and so on. Find other symbols of three in metaphors, words, and ideas. What does three symbolize and why would O. Henry use it throughout this story?

2. O. Henry relishes in paradox. Della and Jim are poverty stricken, yet they are rich in their love for each other. O. Henry also implements irony in his stories. How is irony used in this story?

3. What does Jim's middle name, Dillingham, seem to represent? Use details from the story to support your answer.

4. What is O. Henry trying to tell us when he sets up the Youngs as having little money but wishing to buy expensive presents? Is giving gifts beyond our means as prevailing as it is in this story? Can you give any examples where you have given beyond your means? If so, why did you do if? Is this a good or bad thing?

5. Is O. Henry critical of the Youngs in his assessment of their gift giving? Explain your answer with evidence from the text.

6. A denouement is a literary term that means the final "unknotting" of the plot. A good story has complications, or a "set up," that can only

lead to a satisfactory "pay off." What is the denouement of this story? You will need to explain what the complication of the story is, and how the denouement resolves the complication.

7. O. Henry asserts that Jim and Della are the "Magi" of this story. How is this possible? Explain how symbolism is used to transform Jim and Della of a derelict New York apartment back to the Magi of the East who visit the Christ child.

8. Despite an economical writing style, O. Henry is adept at filling his writing with wonderful images. For example, in the fifth paragraph, O. Henry writes, "She stood by the window and looked out dully at a grey cat walking a grey fence in a grey backyard." Write about the meaning of the preceding paragraph and find others of similar detail for comment (Did you notice the repetition of three?).

9. Word choice plays an important role in understanding story and the author's intent. Consider this from the last part of the story, "And here I have lamely related to you the uneventful chronicle of two foolish **children** in a flat who most **unwisely** sacrificed for each other the greatest treasures of their house. But in a last word **to the wise of these days** let it be said that of all who give gifts **these two were the wisest.**" Why does O. Henry refer to the two protagonists as children? Why would he say "unwisely sacrificed"? Who are "the wise of these days"? If the two "unwisely sacrificed", how are they "the wisest"?

British Short Stories

Oscar Wilde: The Happy Prince (1888)
James Joyce: Araby (1914)
Saki: The Open Window (1914)
Virginia Woolf: A Haunted House (1914)

V

THE HAPPY PRINCE

by Oscar Wilde (1885, Ireland)

- Introduction of the Author
- Synopsis
- Text
- Words & Idioms
- Study Questions

Introduction of the Author: Oscar Wilde (1854-1900)

Though Oscar Wilde lived his later life in controversy and even suffered arrest, he has since been redeemed as an original poet, one of the greatest playwrights of the Victorian Age, and an influence on the youth through his fairy tales.

Wilde was born on October 16, 1854, to a philanthropist father, Sir William Wilde and an educated mother, Francesca Wilde. His father opened a medical clinic for ear and eye disease to the poor and needy, and his mother was a journalist and a poet, writing her poetry under the pseudonym, "Speranza." Oscar was home-schooled as a child and later went on to graduate from Trinity College, Dublin. While in college, his prowess with words surfaced, and he won various awards and scholarships for his works, especially poetry. He fell in love with Florence Balcombe who married Bram Stoker of later *Dracula* fame. The loss of his love was one of the causes for Wilde to leave Ireland and start a successful career as a traveling lecturer in America, London, and Paris from 1881 to 1882.

In 1884, he married Constance Lloyd, an educated woman, and they had two children in succession the following two years. Perhaps forced to make a living for his family, Wilde's greatest efforts followed for the next six years. In 1888 he published a collection of children's fairy tales, *The Happy Prince and Other Tales*. His only novel, *The Picture of Dorian Gray* (1891), was published a year earlier in short story form for an American magazine and was met with critical disappointment, though many consider it a classic now. He followed this with a second collection of children's stories, *The House of Pomegranates* (1892). Though he did publish collections of poetry, Wilde is most famous as a dramatist, his most popular being the witty *The Importance of Being Earnest* (1895).

Out of all his success, Wilde's carefree lifestyle in the Victorian Age was his downfall. First hinted at when he wrote of Shakespeare's famous sonnets being addressed to a boy, Wilde's own sexuality became a scandal as well. Wilde began to have a sexual relationship with a young fan, a seventeen-year-old boy at the time, which set the boy's father off in a rage. The father publicly slandered Wilde, at which point, Wilde sued. The truth of Wilde's homosexuality was eventually brought out in the trial, and Wilde was arrested for it (a crime at the time called "gross indecency"). He was subjected to two years of hard labor, which ruined his health. Upon his release, he changed his name and lived a life of poverty. Three years later, he died of cerebral meningitis in Paris on November 30, 1900.

Wilde may have died in shame, but his work and genius live on as adults and children alike read and respect his writings as true classics.

Synopsis

In a city long ago stood the statue of the Happy Prince that was covered with gold and adorned with precious jewels. The statue of the prince looked happy, but many in the city were not; they looked just like the Happy Prince felt inside, destitute. Like all cities, the rich went about their business indifferent to the plight of the poor.

The statue used to be human and never cared for the poor until his death sent his soul into the statue. The statue of the Happy Prince was an inspiration to all; even the animal kingdom felt inspired by the beautiful statue.

A rather foolish swallow that fell in love with beautiful things in nature became distracted by the statue's beauty and fell in love with it. It made a nest and lived with the Happy Prince. The prince was not happy and cried real tears for the suffering and the poor. His lot in life was to view all the ugliness and misery in and around the city. Though he was clothed in gold and had sapphires for eyes, he could not bear to see the people go without their basic needs.

As winter approached, the swallow felt it was time to fly away to Egypt where it was warm. The Happy Prince asked the bird to take the jewel from his sword and give it to those who needed it the most. He then asked the swallow to tear out his sapphire eyes, and when they were given to the poor, he commanded the swallow to take the gold leafing cov-

ering his body and make sure the poor had food and clothing for the winter. Throughout the long, cold winter, the swallow dreamed of the warmth and wonder of Egypt, yet it helped the statue do good deeds.

The little swallow realized that the worth of life was greater than its own. And though the Happy Prince was now blind, the bird would stay the rest of the winter to fly over the city to be the Prince's eyes and messenger of charity. The cold of winter was too much for the swallow, and it died.

The Happy Prince was eventually torn down due to its ugliness and melted in a fire to be reused as scrap metal. However, its leaden heart would not melt and was thrown out. God ordered two angels to acquire the two most precious items in the city: they brought the dead bird and the leaden heart. They had chosen wisely.

Text

High above the city, on a tall column, stood the statue of the Happy Prince. He was gilded all over with thin leaves of fine gold, for eyes he had two bright sapphires, and a large red ruby glowed on his sword-hilt.

He was very much admired indeed. 'He is as beautiful as a weathercock,' remarked one of the Town Councillors who wished to gain a reputation for having artistic tastes; 'only not quite so useful,' he added, fearing lest people should think him unpractical, which he really was not.

'Why can't you be like the Happy Prince?' asked a sensible mother of her little boy who was crying for the moon. 'The Happy Prince never dreams of crying for anything.'

'I am glad there is some one in the world who is quite

happy,' muttered a disappointed man as he gazed at the wonderful statue.

'He looks just like an angel,' said the Charity Children as they came out of the cathedral in their bright scarlet cloaks, and their clean white pinafores.

'How do you know?' said the Mathematical Master, 'you have never seen one.'

'Ah! but we have, in our dreams,' answered the children; and the Mathematical Master frowned and looked very severe, for he did not approve of children dreaming.

One night there flew over the city a little Swallow. His friends had gone away to Egypt six weeks before, but he had stayed behind, for he was in love with the most beautiful Reed. He had met her early in the spring as he was flying down the river after a big yellow moth, and had been so attracted by her slender waist that he had stopped to talk to her.

'Shall I love you?' said the Swallow, who liked to come to the point at once, and the Reed made him a low bow. So he flew round and round her, touching the water with his wings, and making silver ripples. This was his courtship, and it lasted all through the summer.

'It is a ridiculous attachment,' twittered the other Swallows, 'she has no money, and far too many relations;' and indeed the river was quite full of Reeds. Then, when the autumn came, they all flew away.

After they had gone he felt lonely, and began to tire of his lady-love. 'She has no conversation,' he said, 'and I am afraid that she is a coquette, for she is always flirting with the wind.' And certainly, whenever the wind blew, the Reed made the most graceful curtsies. 'I admit that she is domestic,' he continued, 'but I love travelling, and my wife, consequently, should love travelling also.'

'Will you come away with me?' he said finally to her; but

the Reed shook her head, she was so attached to her home.

'You have been trifling with me,' he cried, 'I am off to the Pyramids. Good-bye!' and he flew away.

All day long he flew, and at night-time he arrived at the city. 'Where shall I put up?' he said; 'I hope the town has made preparations.'

Then he saw the statue on the tall column. 'I will put up there,' he cried; 'it is a fine position with plenty of fresh air.' So he alighted just between the feet of the Happy Prince.

'I have a golden bedroom,' he said softly to himself as he looked round, and he prepared to go to sleep; but just as he was putting his head under his wing a large drop of water fell on him. 'What a curious thing!' he cried, 'there is not a single cloud in the sky, the stars are quite clear and bright, and yet it is raining. The climate in the north of Europe is really dreadful. The Reed used to like the rain, but that was merely her selfishness.'

Then another drop fell.

'What is the use of a statue if it cannot keep the rain off?' he said; 'I must look for a good chimney-pot,' and he determined to fly away.

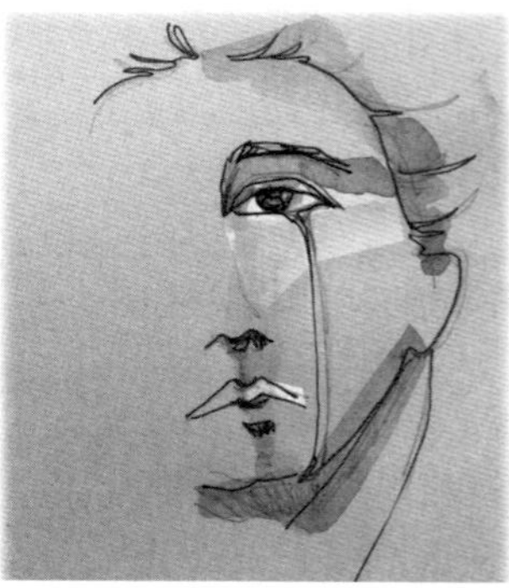

But before he had opened his wings, a third drop fell, and he looked up, and saw - Ah! what did he see?

The eyes of the Happy Prince were filled with tears, and tears were running down his golden cheeks. His face was so beautiful in the moon-light that the little Swallow was filled with pity.

'Who are you?' he said.

'I am the Happy Prince.'

'Why are you weeping then?' asked the Swallow; 'you have quite drenched me.'

'When I was alive and had a human heart,' answered the statue, 'I did not know what tears were, for I lived in the palace of Sans-Souci, where sorrow is not allowed to enter. In the daytime I played with my companions in the garden, and in the evening I led the dance in the Great Hall. Round the garden ran a very lofty wall, but I never cared to ask what lay beyond it, everything about me was so beautiful. My courtiers called me the Happy Prince, and happy indeed I was, if pleasure be happiness. So I lived, and so I died. And now that I am dead they have set me up here so high that I can see all the ugliness and all the misery of my city, and though my heart is made of lead yet I cannot choose but weep.'

'What, is he not solid gold?' said the Swallow to himself. He was too polite to make any personal remarks out loud.

'Far away,' continued the statue in a low musical voice, 'far away in a little street there is a poor house. One of the windows is open, and through it I can see a woman seated at a table. Her face is thin and worn, and she has coarse, red hands, all pricked by the needle, for she is a seamstress. She is embroidering passion-flowers on a satin gown for the loveliest of the Queen's maids-of-honour to wear at the next Court-ball. In a bed in the corner of the room her little boy is lying ill. He has a fever, and is asking for oranges. His mother has nothing to give him but river water, so he is crying. Swallow, Swallow, little Swallow, will you not bring her the ruby out of my sword-hilt? My feet are fastened to this pedestal and I cannot move.'

'I am waited for in Egypt,' said the Swallow. 'My friends are flying up and down the Nile, and talking to the large lotus-flowers. Soon they will go to sleep in the tomb of the great King. The King is there himself in his painted coffin.

He is wrapped in yellow linen, and embalmed with spices. Round his neck is a chain of pale green jade, and his hands are like withered leaves.'

'Swallow, Swallow, little Swallow,' said the Prince, 'will you not stay with me for one night, and be my messenger? The boy is so thirsty, and the mother so sad.'

'I don't think I like boys,' answered the Swallow. 'Last summer, when I was staying on the river, there were two rude boys, the miller's sons, who were always throwing stones at me. They never hit me, of course; we swallows fly far too well for that, and besides, I come of a family famous for its agility; but still, it was a mark of disrespect.'

But the Happy Prince looked so sad that the little Swallow was sorry. 'It is very cold here,' he said; 'but I will stay with you for one night, and be your messenger.'

'Thank you, little Swallow,' said the Prince.

So the Swallow picked out the great ruby from the Prince's sword, and flew away with it in his beak over the roofs of the town.

He passed by the cathedral tower, where the white marble angels were sculptured. He passed by the palace and heard the sound of dancing. A beautiful girl came out on the balcony with her lover. 'How wonderful the stars are,' he said to her, and how wonderful is the power of love!'

'I hope my dress will be ready in time for the State-ball,' she answered; 'I have ordered passion-flowers to be embroidered on it; but the seamstresses are so lazy.'

He passed over the river, and saw the lanterns hanging to the masts of the ships. He passed over the Ghetto, and saw the old Jews bargaining with each other, and weighing out money in copper scales. At last he came to the poor house and looked in. The boy was tossing feverishly on his bed, and the mother had fallen asleep, she was so tired. In he hopped, and laid the great ruby on the table beside the woman's thimble. Then he flew gently round the bed, fanning the boy's forehead with his wings. 'How cool I feel,' said the boy, 'I must be getting better;' and he sank into a delicious slumber.

Then the Swallow flew back to the Happy Prince, and told him what he had done. 'It is curious,' he remarked, 'but I feel quite warm now, although it is so cold.'

'That is because you have done a good action,' said the Prince. And the little Swallow began to think, and then he fell asleep. Thinking always made him sleepy.

When day broke he flew down to the river and had a bath. 'What a remarkable phenomenon,' said the Professor of Ornithology as he was passing over the bridge. 'A swallow in winter!' And he wrote a long letter about it to the local newspaper. Every one quoted it, it was full of so many words that they could not understand.

'To-night I go to Egypt,' said the Swallow, and he was in high spirits at the prospect. He visited all the public monuments, and sat a long time on top of the church steeple. Wherever he went the Sparrows chirruped, and said to each other, 'What a distinguished stranger!' so he enjoyed himself very much.

When the moon rose he flew back to the Happy Prince. 'Have you any commissions for Egypt?' he cried; 'I am just starting.'

'Swallow, Swallow, little Swallow,' said the Prince, 'will you not stay with me one night longer?'

'I am waited for in Egypt,' answered the Swallow. 'To-morrow my friends will fly up to the Second Cataract. The river-horse couches there among the bulrushes, and on a great granite throne sits the God Memnon. All night long he watches the stars, and when the morning star shines he utters one cry of joy, and then he is silent. At noon the yellow lions come down to the water's edge to drink. They have eyes like green beryls, and their roar is louder than the roar of the cataract.'

'Swallow, Swallow, little Swallow,' said the prince, 'far away across the city I see a young man in a garret. He is leaning over a desk covered with papers, and in a tumbler by his side there is a bunch of withered violets. His hair is brown and crisp, and his lips are red as a pomegranate, and he has large and dreamy eyes. He is trying to finish a play for the Director of the Theatre, but he is too cold to write any more. There is no fire in the grate, and hunger has made him faint.'

'I will wait with you one night longer,' said the Swallow, who really had a good heart. 'Shall I take him another ruby?'

'Alas! I have no ruby now,' said the Prince; 'my eyes are all that I have left. They are made of rare sapphires, which were brought out of India a thousand years ago. Pluck out one of them and take it to him. He will sell it to the jewel-

ler, and buy food and firewood, and finish his play.'

'Dear Prince,' said the Swallow, 'I cannot do that;' and he began to weep.

'Swallow, Swallow, little Swallow,' said the Prince, 'do as I command you.'

So the Swallow plucked out the Prince's eye, and flew away to the student's garret. It was easy enough to get in, as there was a hole in the roof. Through this he darted, and came into the room. The young man had his head buried in his hands, so he did not hear the flutter of the bird's wings, and when he looked up he found the beautiful sapphire lying on the withered violets.

'I am beginning to be appreciated,' he cried; 'this is from some great admirer. Now I can finish my play,' and he looked quite happy.

The next day the Swallow flew down to the harbour. He sat on the mast of a large vessel and watched the sailors hauling big chests out of the hold with ropes. 'Heave a-hoy!' they shouted as each chest came up. 'I am going to Egypt!' cried the Swallow, but nobody minded, and when the moon rose he flew back to the Happy Prince.

'I am come to bid you good-bye,' he cried.

'Swallow, Swallow, little Swallow,' said the Prince, 'will you not stay with me one night longer?'

'It is winter,' answered the Swallow, 'and the chill snow will soon be here. In Egypt the sun is warm on the green palm-trees, and the crocodiles lie in the mud and look lazily about them. My companions are building a nest in the Temple of Baalbec, and the pink and white doves are watching them, and cooing to each other. Dear Prince, I must

leave you, but I will never forget you, and next spring I will bring you back two beautiful jewels in place of those you have given away. The ruby shall be redder than a red rose, and the sapphire shall be as blue as the great sea.'

'In the square below,' said the Happy Prince, 'there stands a little match-girl. She has let her matches fall in the gutter, and they are all spoiled. Her father will beat her if she does not bring home some money, and she is crying. She has no shoes or stockings, and her little head is bare. Pluck out my other eye, and give it to her, and her father will not beat her.'

'I will stay with you one night longer,' said the Swallow, 'but I cannot pluck out your eye. You would be quite blind then.'

'Swallow, Swallow, little Swallow,' said the Prince, 'do as I command you.'

So he plucked out the Prince's other eye, and darted down with it. He swooped past the match-girl, and slipped the jewel into the palm of her hand. 'What a lovely bit of glass,' cried the little girl; and she ran home, laughing.

Then the Swallow came back to the Prince. 'You are blind now,' he said, 'so I will stay with you always.'

'No, little Swallow,' said the poor Prince, 'you must go away to Egypt.'

'I will stay with you always,' said the Swallow, and he slept at the Prince's feet.

All the next day he sat on the Prince's shoulder, and told him stories of what he had seen in strange lands. He told him of the red ibises, who stand in long rows on the banks of the Nile, and catch gold fish in their beaks; of the Sphinx, who is as old as the world itself and lives in the desert, and

knows everything; of the merchants, who walk slowly by the side of their camels, and carry amber beads in their hands; of the King of the Mountains of the Moon, who is as black as ebony, and worships a large crystal; of the great green snake that sleeps in a palm-tree, and has twenty priests to feed it with honey-cakes; and of the pygmies who sail over a big lake on large flat leaves, and are always at war with the butterflies.

'Dear little Swallow,' said the Prince, 'you tell me of marvellous things, but more marvellous than anything is the suffering of men and of women. There is no Mystery so great as Misery. Fly over my city, little Swallow, and tell me what you see there.'

So the Swallow flew over the great city, and saw the rich making merry in their beautiful houses, while the beggars were sitting at the gates. He flew into dark lanes, and saw the white faces of starving children looking out listlessly at the black streets. Under the archway of a bridge two little boys were lying in one another's arms to try and keep themselves warm. 'How hungry we are!' they said. 'You must not lie here,' shouted the Watchman, and they wandered out into the rain.

Then he flew back and told the Prince what he had seen.

'I am covered with fine gold,' said the Prince, 'you must take it off, leaf by leaf, and give it to my poor; the living always think that gold can make them happy.'

Leaf after leaf of the fine gold the Swallow picked off, till the Happy Prince looked quite dull and grey. Leaf after leaf of the fine gold he brought to the poor, and the children's faces grew rosier, and they laughed and played games in the street. 'We have bread now!' they cried.

Then the snow came, and after the snow came the frost. The streets looked as if they were made of silver, they were so bright and glistening; long icicles like crystal daggers hung down from the eaves of the houses, everybody went about in furs, and the little boys wore scarlet caps and skated on the ice.

The poor little Swallow grew colder and colder, but he would not leave the Prince, he loved him too well. He picked up

crumbs outside the baker's door where the baker was not looking, and tried to keep himself warm by flapping his wings.

But at last he knew that he was going to die. He had just strength to fly up to the Prince's shoulder once more. 'Good-bye, dear Prince!' he murmured, 'will you let me kiss your hand?'

'I am glad that you are going to Egypt at last, little Swallow,' said the Prince, 'you have stayed too long here; but you must kiss me on the lips, for I love you.'

'It is not to Egypt that I am going,' said the Swallow. 'I am going to the House of Death. Death is the brother of Sleep, is he not?'

And he kissed the Happy Prince on the lips, and fell down dead at his feet.

At that moment a curious crack sounded inside the statue, as if something had broken. The fact is that the leaden heart had snapped right in two. It certainly was a dreadfully hard frost. Early the next morning the Mayor was walking in the square below in company with the Town Councillors. As they passed the column he looked up at the statue: 'Dear me! how shabby the Happy Prince looks!' he said.

'How shabby indeed!' cried the Town Councillors, who always agreed with the Mayor, and they went up to look at it.

'The ruby has fallen out of his sword, his eyes are gone, and he is golden no longer,' said the Mayor; 'in fact, he is little better than a beggar!'

'Little better than a beggar' said the Town Councillors.

'And here is actually a dead bird at his feet!' continued the Mayor. 'We must really issue a proclamation that birds are not to be allowed to die here.' And the Town Clerk made a note of the suggestion.

So they pulled down the statue of the Happy Prince. 'As he is no longer beautiful he is no longer useful,' said the Art Professor at the University.

Then they melted the statue in a furnace, and the Mayor held a meeting of the Corporation to decide what was to be done with the metal. 'We must have another statue, of course,' he said, 'and it shall be a statue of myself.'

'Of myself,' said each of the Town Councillors, and they quarrelled. When I last heard of them they were quarrelling still.

'What a strange thing!' said the overseer of the workmen at the foundry. 'This broken lead heart will not melt in the furnace. We must throw it away.' So they threw it on a dust-heap where the dead Swallow was also lying.

'Bring me the two most precious things in the city,' said God to one of His Angels; and the Angel brought Him the leaden heart and the dead bird.

'You have rightly chosen,' said God, 'for in my garden of Paradise this little bird shall sing for evermore, and in my city of gold the Happy Prince shall praise me.'

Words & Idioms

alas! (interj) an expression used when sad or disappointed.
Baalbec: (n) a Syrian city in Biblical times now destroyed.
beryl: (n) a precious stone or gem usually the color of white, green, blue, yellow, or pink.
bulrush: (n) a tall grass-like plant that grows in clusters in marshes, similar to a reed.
Cataract: (n) a large waterfall found on the Nile.
chimney-pot: (n) a metal pipe added to the top of a chimney.
chirrup: (v) the chirping sound a bird makes.
commission: (n) asking to carry out a certain job.
coo: (v) (the sound a dove or pigeon makes.
coquette: (n) a flirtatious woman.
courtiers: (n) people who attend a king's court. Entourage is the modern term.
curtsey: (n) the type of bow a female makes by bending the knees with one foot forward and holding the dress out to the side with both hands.
dart: (v) a sudden or fast movement as if throwing a dart.
distinguished: (adj.) excellent; well-known in a positive way.
drench: (v) to get completely wet.
eaves: (n) the part of the roof that hangs over the bottom edge, usually to catch water.
ebony: (adj) very dark brown or black.
embalm: (v) to replace the blood in a dead body with a preservative liquid.
embroider: (v) to make (clothing, rugs) through needlecraft.
foundry: (n) a place where metal is melted and worked into various shapes.

garret: (n) a dismal room located in the top part of a house, similar to an attic.

ghetto: (n) the old part of a city that is run down and occupied by minority groups.

gilded: (v) to cover with gold

glisten: (v) to sparkle in the sunlight.

grate: (n) an older word for fireplace.

geave a-hoy: an expression used to tell someone to pull hard on a rope, especially sailors.

ibis: (n) a type of bird found in Egypt that has a narrow curving beak.

listlessly: (adv) without energy.

Memnon: (n) a demigod of Persia.

miller: (n) a worker in a mill (a place that grinds wheat).

ornithology: (n) related to the study of birds.

pinafore: (n) a type of sleeveless apron that small girls usually wear over a dress.

pluck: (v) to remove with the fingers (or, in this case, a beak).

prospect: (n) the possibility that something planned will happen.

Pygmies: (pl. n) a mythological race of small creatures similar to fairies, but lacking wings.

Sans-Souci: (n) either a fictional palace or perhaps a palace built (1745-47) at Potsdam, Germany, by Frederick II.

Second Cataract: (n) the second waterfall found on the Nile near Nubia (south Egypt).

shabby: (adj) old and worn out.

steeple: (n) the tallest point or tower on a church.

swallow: (n) a small, swift flying bird usually with a forked tail.

thimble: (n) a small cup that fits on the finger; it is used while sewing.
trifle: (v) to not take a subject seriously; a joke or a jest.
twitter: (v) to laugh at or tease, especially when someone does something embarrassing.
weathercock: (n) a weather vane in the shape of rooster that showed the direction of the wind and usually sat on top of a barn.
withered: (adj) to be dried up and shrunken.

Study Questions

1. This is one of the rare works of fiction that is written in fairy tale form. What makes this story read like a fairy tale compared to the other stories?

2. The Grimm fairy tales were often dark and ended badly for the protagonists. After the modern fairy tales of Wilde and others were made popular, Grimm's fairy tales were altered to more favorable endings. If you compare Wilde's fairy tales, which are considered some of the original fairy tales in English, with the fairy tales made popular by the Brothers Grimm about a half a century earlier, what makes this story different from the earlier ones?

   Visit http://www.cs.cmu.edu/~spok/grimmtmp/ to review various Grimm Brothers' fairy tales

3. *The Happy Prince* can also be read as an allegory: an extended metaphor where the characters have meanings outside the actual story. Reread the story. The story tells of a statue and a bird. What is Wilde actually talking about outside the story (this is the allegory of the story)? Who or what do the Mayor and Town Councillors represent? The Professor of Ornithology? The Town Clerk? The Art Professor?

4. Why does Wilde have his birds fly away to Egypt? What is the significance of mentioning Egypt and all its wonders in the tale?

5. What is the meaning of having the prince turn into a statue and having a heart of lead that would not melt and then tossed into the trash?

6. What role does the swallow play in this tale? How important is it to have a swallow in the plot? Could it have been another animal? Why or why not? What is the allegorical meaning behind the swallow?

VI

ARABY

by James Joyce (1914, Ireland)

- Introduction of the Author
- Synopsis
- Text
- Words & Idioms
- Study Questions

Introduction of the Author: James Joyce (1882-1941)

Hailed as one of the greatest writers of the 20th century, James Joyce was born in Dublin, Ireland on February 2, 1882, the oldest of ten children. He was raised by a father, who was known to waste money, and a devout Catholic mother. By the age of six, he was sent to Belvedere College for a Catholic education under Jesuit priests with the hopes that he would later become a priest. Living in Ireland that sought constant liberation from British rule, Joyce eventually left his country, needing to distance himself from what he considered a losing battle. Though he lived in poverty as an English teacher in several countries, he wrote every day and, perhaps out of homesickness, often returned to the city of his birth in his works of fiction with such delicate detail that a reader who has never visited Dublin would intimately know of all its features. He collected his short stories in his first publication, *Dubliners* (1914).

James Joyce is considered the father of **stream-of-consciousness**, a literary form where the author strays as far away from the rules of normal writing to the point where the reader is given the sense that he or she is "reading" the mind of the narrator. Punctuation, quotation marks, and other conventional forms of grammar may be removed to add to the effect. Since the mind wanders as it thinks freely, so does the text of the narrator, often creating confusion. *Dubliners*, which includes the short story "Araby," started to exhibit early forms of stream-of-consciousness, but not until his semi-autobiographical novel *A Portrait of the Artist as a Young Man* (1914), and his literary masterpiece

Ulysses, (1922) did it get used fully. *Ulysses* also started out as a short story to be featured in *Dubliners*, but the idea of expanding the narrative to include the daily life of a man as an anti-heroic journey in imitation of Homer's Odyssey turned into a 700+ page book.

Ulysses covered the day in the life of a man while his next great work of fiction covered the dream ridden haunts of the night in *Finnegan's Wake* (1939). Taking over 17 years to write, Joyce hailed it as the greatest achievement of his profession, having discarded all plot devices and employing stream-of-consciousness to the maximum. During the writing of this book, Joyce started to go blind. He had close friends write what he dictated, much the way the blind Milton would dictate *Paradise Lost*. Joyce also suffered from stomach cramps before its publication. When it was published, the literary world did not know what to make of it. Only with the study and understanding of stream-of-consciousness could the genius of the work be understood.

As World War II swept through Europe, Joyce feared that all he had worked for would be lost when France, where he was living at the time, became occupied by the Nazis. He was forced to move to Zurich, Switzerland, where his stomach pains continued. On January 13, 1941, after an operation to remove an ulcer, he quietly passed away after saying his goodbyes to his loved ones. He was 51. Joyce may have died in his writing prime, but the legacy he left behind changed the way we would read and write fiction.

Synopsis

The unnamed narrator of the story relates the memory of his first love and a rather simple quest he sets off on to win her affections. His quest starts when he sees the sister of one of his friends standing on the porch in their neighborhood' s quiet street. The narrator has secretly held affection for the girl, and since they are neighbors, he would watch her from afar. Being a shy boy, he dares not speak to her and only professes his love for her in his heart.

The day she speaks to him is like receiving a call from a goddess. She simply asks him if he is going to Araby, "a splendid bazaar," and mentions that she cannot go because she has a church trip that day. Like a knight before the queen, the narrator promises to bring her back something from the eastern style fair. The rest of the day, he cannot eat, sleep, or study without thinking about her or the promise he made. He asks his aunt and uncle for permission to go to the bazaar, which they give. The rest of the day passes in a blur until he returns from school.

The only problem is he has to wait for his uncle to return from work to get money to buy his promised gift, and his uncle is late. As the evening wears on without any sign of his Uncle, the boy endures a torture befitting a questing knight, and he may not even make it to the bazaar before it closes. His uncle finally returns; he had forgotten his promise, and begrudgingly gives the boy money.

Racing all the way to the fair, the boy finds himself in a labyrinth of shops. Walking around in such a strange world, he is entranced by the people and the wares. His heart sinks when he realizes the great worth of the treasures in the stalls. Before he reaches the middle of the market, the lights go out as the shops close for the night. The story ends with the narrator recognizing his failure in the quest through grief and irritation.

But is our little hero defeated?

Text

North Richmond Street, being blind, was a quiet street except at the hour when the Christian Brothers' School set the boys free. An uninhabited house of two stories stood at the blind end, detached from its neighbours in a square ground. The other houses of the street, conscious of decent lives within them, gazed at one another with brown imperturbable faces.

The former tenant of our house, a priest, had died in the back drawing-room. Air, musty from having been long enclosed, hung in all the rooms, and the waste room behind the kitchen was littered with old useless papers. Among these I found a few paper-covered books, the pages of which were curled and damp: *The Abbot*, by Walter Scott, *The Devout Communicant*, and *The Memoirs of Vidocq*. I liked the last best because its leaves were yellow. The wild garden behind the house contained a central apple-tree and a few straggling bushes, under one of which I found the late tenant's rusty bicycle-pump. He had been a very charitable priest; in his will he had left all his money to institutions and the furniture of his house to his sister.

When the short days of winter came, dusk fell before we had well eaten our dinners. When we met in the street the houses had grown sombre. The space of sky above us was the colour of ever-changing violet and towards it the lamps of the street lifted their feeble lanterns. The cold air stung us and we played

till our bodies glowed. Our shouts echoed in the silent street. The career of our play brought us through the dark muddy lanes behind the houses, where we ran the gauntlet of the rough tribes from the cottages, to the back doors of the dark dripping gardens where odours arose from the ashpits, to the dark odorous stables where a coachman smoothed and combed the horse or shook music from the buckled harness. When we returned to the street, light from the kitchen windows had filled the areas. If my uncle was seen turning the corner, we hid in the shadow until we had seen him safely housed. Or if Mangan's sister came out on the doorstep to call her brother in to his tea, we watched her from our shadow peer up and down the street. We waited to see whether she would remain or go in and, if she remained, we left our shadow and walked up to Mangan's steps resignedly. She was waiting for us, her figure defined by the light from the half-opened door. Her brother always teased her before he obeyed, and I stood by the railings looking at her. Her dress swung as she moved her body, and the soft rope of her hair tossed from side to side.

Every morning I lay on the floor in the front parlour watching her door. The blind was pulled down to within an inch of the sash so that I could not be seen. When she came out on the doorstep my heart leaped. I ran to the hall, seized my books and followed her. I kept her brown figure always in my eye and, when we came near the point at which our ways diverged, I quickened my pace and passed her. This happened morning after morning. I had never spoken to her, except for a few casual words, and yet her name was like a summons to all my foolish blood.

Her image accompanied me even in places the most hostile to romance. On Saturday evenings when my aunt went marketing I had to go to carry some of the parcels. We walked through the flaring streets, jostled by drunken men and bargaining women, amid the curses of labourers, the shrill litanies of shop-boys who stood on guard by the barrels of pigs' cheeks, the nasal chanting of street- singers, who sang a come-all-you about O'Donovan Rossa, or a ballad about the troubles in our native land. These noises converged in a single sensation of life for me: I imagined that I bore my chalice safely through a throng of foes. Her name sprang to my lips at moments in strange prayers and praises which I myself did not understand. My eyes were often full of tears (I could not tell why) and at times a flood from my heart seemed to pour itself out into my bosom. I thought little of the future. I did not know whether I would ever speak to her or not or, if I spoke to her, how I could tell her of my confused adoration. But my body was like a harp and her words and gestures were like fingers running upon the wires.

One evening I went into the back drawing-room in which the priest had died. It was a dark rainy evening and there was no sound in the house. Through one of the broken panes I heard the rain impinge upon the earth, the fine incessant needles of water playing in the sodden beds. Some distant lamp or lighted window gleamed below me. I was thankful that I could see so little. All my senses seemed to desire to veil themselves and, feeling that I was about to slip from them, I pressed the palms of my hands together until they trem-

bled, murmuring: 'O love! O love!' many times.

At last she spoke to me. When she addressed the first words to me I was so confused that I did not know what to answer. She asked me was I going to Araby. I forgot whether I answered yes or no. It would be a splendid bazaar; she said she would love to go.

'And why can't you?' I asked.

While she spoke she turned a silver bracelet round and round her wrist. She could not go, she said, because there would be a retreat that week in her convent. Her brother and two other boys were fighting for their caps, and I was alone at the railings. She held one of the spikes, bowing her head towards me. The light from the lamp opposite our door caught the white curve of her neck, lit up her hair that rested there and, falling, lit up the hand upon the railing. It fell over one side of her dress and caught the white border of a petticoat, just visible as she stood at ease.

'It's well for you,' she said.

'If I go,' I said, 'I will bring you something.'

What innumerable follies laid waste my waking and sleeping thoughts after that evening! I wished to annihilate the tedious intervening days. I chafed against the work of school. At night in my bedroom and by day in the classroom her image came between me and the page I strove to read. The syllables of the word Araby were called to me through the silence in which my soul luxuriated and cast an Eastern enchantment over me. I asked for leave to go to the bazaar on Saturday night. My aunt was surprised, and hoped it was not some Freemason affair. I answered few questions in class. I watched my master's face pass from amiability to sternness; he hoped I was not beginning to idle. I could not call my wandering thoughts together. I had hardly any patience with the serious work of life which, now that it stood between me and my desire, seemed to me child's play, ugly monotonous child's play.

On Saturday morning I reminded my uncle that I wished to go to the bazaar in the evening. He was fussing at the hallstand, looking for the hat-brush, and answered me curtly:

'Yes, boy, I know.'

As he was in the hall I could not go into the front parlour and lie at the window. I felt the house in bad humour and walked slowly towards the school. The air was pitilessly raw and already my heart misgave me.

When I came home to dinner my uncle had not yet been home. Still it was early. I sat staring at the clock for some time and, when its ticking began to irritate me, I left the room. I mounted the staircase and gained the upper part of the house. The high, cold, empty, gloomy rooms liberated me and I went from room to room singing. From the front window I saw my companions playing below in the street. Their cries reached me weakened and indistinct and, leaning my forehead against the cool glass, I looked over at the dark house where she lived. I may have stood there for an hour, seeing nothing but the brown-clad figure cast by my imagination, touched discreetly by the lamplight at the curved neck, at the hand upon the railings and at the border below the dress.

When I came downstairs again I found Mrs Mercer sitting at the fire. She was an old, garrulous woman, a pawnbroker's widow, who collected used stamps for some pious purpose. I had to endure the gossip of the tea-table. The meal was prolonged beyond an hour and still my uncle did not come. Mrs Mercer stood up to go: she was sorry she couldn't wait any longer, but it was after eight o'clock and she did not like to be out late, as the night air was bad for her. When she had gone I began to walk up and down the room, clenching my fists. My aunt said:

'I'm afraid you may put off your bazaar for this night of Our Lord.'

At nine o'clock I heard my uncle's latchkey in the hall door. I heard him talking to himself and heard the hallstand rocking when it had received the weight of his overcoat. I could interpret these signs. When he was midway through his dinner I asked him to give me the money to go to the bazaar. He had forgotten.

'The people are in bed and after their first sleep now,' he said.

I did not smile. My aunt said to him energetically:

'Can't you give him the money and let him go? You've kept him late enough as it is.'

My uncle said he was very sorry he had forgotten. He said he believed in the old saying: 'All work and no play makes Jack a dull boy.' He asked me where I was going and, when I told him a second time, he asked me did I know The Arab's Farewell to his Steed. When I left the kitchen he was about to recite the opening lines of the piece to my aunt.

I held a florin tightly in my hand as I strode down Buckingham Street towards the station. The sight of the streets thronged with buyers and glaring with gas recalled to me the purpose of my journey. I took my seat in a third-class carriage of a deserted train. After an intolerable delay the train moved out of the station slowly. It crept

onward among ruinous houses and over the twinkling river. At Westland Row Station a crowd of people pressed to the carriage doors; but the porters moved them back, saying that it was a special train for the bazaar. I remained alone in the bare carriage. In a few minutes the train drew up beside an improvised wooden platform. I passed out on to the road and saw by the lighted dial of a clock that it was ten minutes to ten. In front of me was a large building which displayed the magical name.

I could not find any sixpenny entrance and, fearing that the bazaar would be closed, I passed in quickly through a turnstile, handing a shilling to a weary-looking man. I found myself in a big hall girded at half its height by a gallery. Nearly all the stalls were closed and the greater part of the hall was in darkness. I recognized a silence like that which pervades a church after a service. I walked into the centre of the bazaar timidly. A few people were gathered about the stalls which were still open. Before a curtain, over which the words Café Chantantwere written in coloured lamps, two men were counting money on a salver. I listened to the fall of the coins.

Remembering with difficulty why I had come, I went over to one of the stalls and examined porcelain vases and flowered tea-sets. At the door of the stall a young lady was talking and laughing with two young gentlemen. I remarked their English accents and listened vaguely to their conversation.

'O, I never said such a thing!'

'O, but you did!'

'O, but I didn't!'

'Didn't she say that?'

'Yes. I heard her.'

'O, there's a... fib!'

Observing me, the young lady came over and asked me did I wish to buy anything. The tone of her voice was not encouraging; she seemed to have spoken to me out of a sense of duty. I looked humbly at the great jars that stood like eastern guards at either side of the dark entrance to the stall and murmured:

'No, thank you.'

The young lady changed the position of one of the vases and went back to the two young men. They began to talk of the same subject. Once or twice the young lady glanced at me over her shoulder.

I lingered before her stall, though I knew my stay was useless, to make my interest in her wares seem the more real. Then I turned away slowly and walked down the middle of the bazaar. I allowed the two pennies to fall against the sixpence in my pocket. I heard a voice call from one end of the gallery that the light was out. The upper part of the hall was now completely dark.

Gazing up into the darkness I saw myself as a creature driven and derided by vanity; and my eyes burned with anguish and anger.

Words & Idioms

amiability: (adj) friendly and likable.
ashpit: (n) a hole beneath a fireplace where the ashes fall; an ash-hole.
bazaar: (n) an outdoor market with shops and stalls along the street.
chafed: (v) to become annoyed.
convent: (n) a church or building where nuns live.
deride: (v) mock, make fun of.
drawing-room: (n) a room in a house where a group goes to after a dinner to smoke and talk.
florin: (n) a British coin worth two shillings (see shilling).
folly: (v) to do something foolish usually with a negative outcome.
garrulous: (adj) talkative; always talking without stopping.
gauntlet: (n) a difficult trial or ordeal.
hallstand: (n) a piece of furniture in the hallway where hats, coats, and umbrellas are hung.
harness: (n) gear that is strapped to horse to pull a carriage.
humour: (n) an old fashioned British word for feeling or mood.
imperturbable: (adj) calm, unable to be excited.
impinge: (v) to collide or hit.
incessant: (adj) continuous without pause.
litany: (n) a chant or a song that is continuous.
luxuriate: (v) to spoil oneself.
odorous: (adj) having a particular smell.
parlour: (n) a room in a house where people can sit and relax.
pawnbroker: (n) a person that lends money in exchange for personal property.

pervade: (v) to exist in the surrounding area.

petticoat: (n) a female underskirt usually trimmed with lace.

pious: (adj) religious.

resignedly: (adv) with a feeling of giving up.

run the gauntlet: to go through a difficult maze that is often full of danger.

salver: (n) a tray.

sash: (n) a window frame

shilling: (n) A British coin worth one twentieth of a pound, 5 new pence, or 12 old pence before 1971.

sixpenny: (adj) cheap.

sodden: (adj) to be completely wet.

sombre: (adj) dark and gloomy.

tenant: (n) a person that lives a house or apartment.

The Arab's Farewell to his Steed: a short story by Caroline Norton (1808-1887).

Vidocq: the legendary French Detective, not fictitious.

Study Questions

1. How is this story like the quest of a knight? What are the trials he must endure to reach his goal?

2. What kind of a person is the narrator? Though his age is not given, how old do you think he is?

3. What purpose does the use of light serve in the character description of Mangan's sister?

4. What role does the Uncle play in the story?

5. Does the boy hold real love for Mangan's sister, or is it just an infatuation? Use evidence from the story to explain your answer.

6. Is there anything heroic about the narrator? What is or is not heroic about him?

7. The story has great setting descriptions that help us to see the narrator's world. What are some images that stick out in your mind? Why are these so memorable?

8. Is this a light or dark story? Is the boy successful in his journey? Even if he does not gain the "treasure" for Mangan's sister, does he gain anything else? If so, what is it?

9. If the narrator is so fond of Mangan's sister, why doesn't he ever mention her name? What does this tell us about his "love" for her?

VII

THE OPEN WINDOW

by Saki (1914, England)

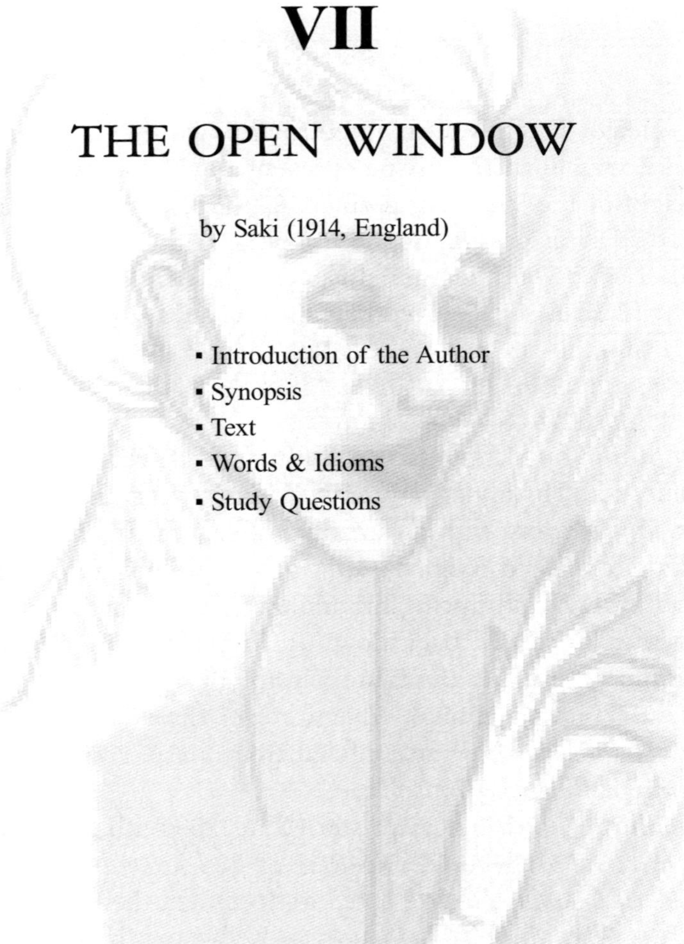

- Introduction of the Author
- Synopsis
- Text
- Words & Idioms
- Study Questions

Introduction of the Author: Saki (1870-1916)

Hector Hugh Munro, famously known by his pen name Saki, was born in Burma (present day Myanmar) at the height of the Victorian period (1837-1901), which was a period of great prosperity and the peak of the British Empire. His father was the chief inspector for the Burma police. The Munros soon moved back to England, where his father left him, his mother, and his two siblings in the care of two aunts before he left for India. Munro's mother was killed by a stampeding cow when he was two.

Munro's strict aunts raised him, and he received a good education. His father only visited once a year, and his childhood was overseen by women who were far from maternal. His father liked to travel, so Munro saw France, Germany, and Switzerland during his adolescence. Though his father eventually settled back down in England to be a teacher, Munro returned to Burma to join the Burma police when he was 23. Having enough adventure for three years—he was never a healthy boy and suffered from malaria—he returned to England to be a journalist.

Munro's writing career started in 1900 with the publication of his first book, *The Rise of the Russian Empire*, a historical study that attempted to document the Russian Empire as Edward Gibbon successfully did for the Romans in *The Decline and Fall of the Roman Empire* (1788). Munro's work failed to inspire as its predecessor did, and critics even ridiculed it in America. Luckily, Munro still had his day job, and being a journalist allowed him to see Europe, which influenced his fiction writing later. He covered the upheavals in the Balkans (1902) and Warsaw (1904), and the revolution in St. Petersburg (1905). He eventually moved to Paris in 1907.

Turning to fiction instead, Monroe wrote several short stories for newspapers and collected them in *Not-So-Stories* (1902). Monroe took the pen name Saki, which he used on all his newspaper correspondents and short stories. The name Saki comes from the *Rubaiyat of Omar Khayyam*, a collection of Persian poems from the twelfth century. In the poem, Saki means cupbearer in Farsi, the language of Iran: "And fear not lest Existence closing your / Account, and mine, should know the me no more; / The Eternal Saki from that Bowl has pour'd / millions of Bubbles like us, and will pour." Like the meaning of his name, Munro, too, would be the cup bearer of stories poured forth for many to enjoy.

With the advent of King Edward VII upon Queen Victoria's death in 1901, a new era, the Edwardian Period, started and was seen by many as a Golden Age of opulence for the rich. However, it was overwrought with lethargy and mediocrity, of which Munro was a scathing critic, often using witty satire.

In 1911, he published another collection of short stories *The Chronicles of Clovis*, which also has stories criticized as being anti-Semitic and misogynistic. His first novel, *The Unbearable Bassington*, was written shortly after. 1914 marked the year he published *Beasts and Super-Beasts*, a collection of short stories that contains his most often anthologized and popular story "The Open Window." Like all his previous works, the writing is simple, yet his cynicism and wit are as sharp as ever. The popularity and style of his stories have been compared with those of O. Henry.

He wrote his second novel, *When William Came*, in 1913, a type of alternate history novel which speculated that British society fell under the invasion of a German emperor

named William II. Written before the outbreak of the World War I, the novel is an example of the invasion literature popular at that time, made ever popular by the likes of H.G. Wells, and predicted the German aggression leading to a worldwide conflict.

When the Great War did break out in 1914, Munro enlisted in the army, though he was not required to do so due to his age. On November 14, two years later, he was fighting in the trenches near the northern tip of France, where he was huddling in a shell crater and enemy fire zipping past his head. A sniper's bullet eventually caught him, and he died, another tragic victim of the war.

Synopsis

Framton Nuttel has just moved into a quiet neighborhood. He is suffering from a nervous breakdown and is in need of a peaceful life. In Edwardian polite society, it is common for people who wished to settle into new neighborhoods to visit their neighbors with a letter of introduction from a mutual acquaintance. So, Mr. Nuttel visits Mrs. Sappleton and her niece to introduce himself and to present his letter of introduction written by his sister.

Mrs. Sappleton is not present, but he can speak to her niece, Vera. When Vera finds out that he knows no one in the area or her aunt, she proceeds to tell him a story, a tragedy about her aunt. He is initially surprised that a tragedy could occur in such a restful, country area, but he listens with growing concern.

Three years ago, before Mr. Nuttel's sister even visited the area, Mrs. Sappleton's husband and two sons went hunting. They exited through a large French window that opens out the back of the house to shoot some snipe. Since they live close to a bog and it was a particularly wet summer, the three men got lost, and their bodies were never found.

Mrs. Sappleton never recovered from the tragedy, and she still hopes to this day that her husband and two sons will return through the very French window they exited with their hunting dog. Thus, the reason she keeps the large window open daily until the sun sets.

Vera is quite particular about her father taking a white rain coat with him and the son singing a "Bertie" song on the day they disappeared.

Mrs. Sappleton enters with apologies for being late soon after Vera finishes her story. She also apologizes about the open window since she expects her husband and son to return soon after their snipe hunting.

Feeling uncomfortable about hearing Mrs. Sappleton talk of the dead as if they are alive, Mr. Nuttel tries to change the subject several times. However, she does not seem to notice his efforts, for as she talks, she keeps looking over at the open window as if the men will return any minute.

Mr. Nuttel finally distracts her long enough with talk of his failing health and how he must avoid all physical and mental strains.

It is then that Mrs. Sappleton jumps up to announce the arrival of her hunters. Shivering, Mr. Nuttel looks over at Vera for confirmation of Mrs. Sappleton's mental problem only to see her looking at the open window with eyes full of horror.

He turns to see what should cause her such a scare and sees three shadowy men walking out of the fog with guns in their hands and a hunting dog at their heels. One is carrying a white rain coat, and the other is singing about Bertie.

Mr. Nuttel leaps to his feet, grabs his coat and cane, and rushes out of the house onto the road, narrowly avoiding a bicyclist.

Mr. Sappleton and his two sons enter through the open French window, asking about the man that had just left in a hurry.

Mrs. Sappleton found him rather peculiar since all he could talk about was his illnesses and then leave without saying goodbye.

Vera thinks the dog scared Mr. Nuttel since he is afraid of them. She explains that Mr. Nuttel was in India and a pack of wild dogs hunted him into a cemetery. He had to spend the night in a freshly dug grave with the dogs standing over him snarling and barking.

Vera always tells stories that are not true. Always.

Text

My aunt will be down presently, Mr. Nuttel," said a very self-possessed young lady of fifteen; "in the meantime you must try and put up with me."

Framton Nuttel endeavoured to say the correct something which should duly flatter the niece of the moment without unduly discounting the aunt that was to come. Privately he doubted more than ever whether these formal visits on a succession of total strangers would do much towards helping the nerve cure which he was supposed to be undergoing.

"I know how it will be," his sister had said when he was preparing to migrate to this rural retreat; "you will bury yourself down there and not speak to a living soul, and your nerves will be worse than ever from moping. I shall just give you letters of introduction to all the people I know there. Some of them, as far as I can remember, were quite nice."

Framton wondered whether Mrs. Sappleton, the lady to whom he was presenting one of the letters of introduction came into the nice division.

"Do you know many of the people round here?" asked the niece, when she judged that they had had sufficient silent communion.

"Hardly a soul," said Framton. "My sister was staying here, at the rectory, you know, some four years ago, and she gave me letters of introduction to some of the people here."

He made the last statement in a tone of distinct regret.

"Then you know practically nothing about my aunt?"

pursued the self-possessed young lady.

“Only her name and address,” admitted the caller. He was wondering whether Mrs. Sappleton was in the married or widowed state. An undefinable something about the room seemed to suggest masculine habitation.

“Her great tragedy happened just three years ago,” said the child; “that would be since your sister’s time.”

“Her tragedy?” asked Framton; somehow in this restful country spot tragedies seemed out of place.

< 2 >

“You may wonder why we keep that window wide open on an October afternoon,” said the niece, indicating a large French window that opened on to a lawn.

“It is quite warm for the time of the year,” said Framton; “but has that window got anything to do with the tragedy?”

“Out through that window, three years ago to a day, her husband and her two young brothers went off for their day’ s shooting. They never came back. In crossing the moor to their favourite snipe-shooting ground they were all three engulfed in a treacherous piece of bog. It had been that dreadful wet summer, you know, and places that were safe in other years gave way suddenly without warning. Their bodies were never recovered. That was the dreadful part of it.” Here the child’s voice lost its self-possessed note and became falteringly human. “Poor aunt always thinks that they will come back someday, they and the little brown spaniel that was lost with them, and walk in at that window just as they used to do. That is why the window is kept open every evening till it is quite dusk. Poor dear aunt, she has often told me how they went out, her husband with his white waterproof coat over his arm, and Ronnie, her youngest brother, singing 'Bertie, why do you bound?' as he always did to tease her, because she said it got on her nerves. Do you know, sometimes on still, quiet evenings like this, I almost get a creepy feeling that they will all walk in through that window –"

She broke off with a little shudder. It was a relief to Framton when the aunt bustled into the room with a whirl of apologies for being late in making her appearance.

"I hope Vera has been amusing you?" she said.

"She has been very interesting," said Framton.

"I hope you don't mind the open window," said Mrs. Sappleton briskly; "my husband and brothers will be home directly from shooting, and they always come in this way.

They've been out for snipe in the marshes today, so they'll make a fine mess over my poor carpets. So like you menfolk, isn't it?"

< 3 >

She rattled on cheerfully about the shooting and the scarcity of birds, and the prospects for duck in the winter. To Framton it was all purely horrible. He made a desperate but only partially successful effort to turn the talk on to a less ghastly topic, he was conscious that his hostess was giving him only a fragment of her attention, and her eyes were constantly straying past him to the open window and the lawn beyond. It was certainly an unfortunate coincidence that he should have paid his visit on this tragic anniversary.

"The doctors agree in ordering me complete rest, an absence of mental excitement, and avoidance of anything in the nature of violent physical exercise," announced Framton, who laboured under the tolerably widespread delusion that total strangers and chance acquaintances are hungry for the least detail of one's ailments and infirmities, their cause and cure. "On the matter of diet they are not so much in agreement," he continued.

"No?" said Mrs. Sappleton, in a voice which only replaced a yawn at the last moment. Then she suddenly brightened into alert attention - but not to what Framton was saying.

"Here they are at last!" she cried. "Just in time for tea, and don't they look as if they were muddy up to the eyes!"

Framton shivered slightly and turned towards the niece with a look intended to convey sympathetic comprehension. The child was staring out through the open window with a dazed horror in her eyes. In a chill shock of nameless fear Framton swung round in his seat and looked in the same direction.

In the deepening twilight three figures were walking across the lawn towards the window, they all carried guns under their arms, and one of them was additionally burdened with a white coat hung over his shoulders. A tired brown spaniel kept close at their heels. Noiselessly they neared the house, and then a hoarse young voice chanted out of the dusk: "I said, Bertie, why do you bound?"

Framton grabbed wildly at his stick and hat; the hall door, the gravel drive, and the front gate were dimly noted stages in his headlong retreat. A cyclist coming along the road had to run into the hedge to avoid imminent collision.

< 4 >

"Here we are, my dear," said the bearer of the white mackintosh, coming in through the window, "fairly muddy, but most of it's dry. Who was that who bolted out as we came up?"

"A most extraordinary man, a Mr. Nuttel," said Mrs. Sappleton; "could only talk about his illnesses, and dashed off without a word of goodby or apology when you arrived. One would think he had seen a ghost."

"I expect it was the spaniel," said the niece calmly; "he told me he had a horror of dogs. He was once hunted into a cemetery somewhere on the banks of the Ganges by a pack of pariah dogs, and had to spend the night in a newly dug grave with the creatures snarling and grinning and foaming just above him. Enough to make anyone lose their nerve."

Romance at short notice was her specialty.

Words & Idioms

bog: (n) grassy area saturated with water so that it becomes spongy and swampy
communion: (n) speaking
duly: (adv) properly
endevour: (v) to make an effort; try
Ganges: (n) a large river that flows through Northern India
gravel-drive: (n) the gravel driveway (as opposed to a dirt one) that leads from the main road up to a house
mackintosh: (n) raincoat
moor: (n) marsh
moping: (adj) sulking; in depression
pariah dogs: (n. phr) dogs that have been abandoned and turned wild
rectory: (n) a building of a local Christian leader large enough to house his family and other boarders
snipe: (n) a small game bird with a long, pointed bill
spaniel: (n) a small bird hunting dog

Study Questions

1. A story must have a protagonist and an antagonist. Who is the protagonist of this story? Why?

2. Who is the antagonist in this story? Why?

3. Who is the most interesting and least interesting person in this story, Vera or Mr. Nuttel? Why?

4. Is the most interesting person the protagonist or antagonist? Is the least interesting person the protagonist or antagonist?

5. Do you know anybody who is like Vera in this story? How so? How about Mr. Nuttel?

---

6. What kind of personality do you think the girl has?

7. What is the difference between telling stories that Saki tells and the stories the girl tells? Is there a difference? Why or why not?

8. Can fiction, or even news reporting, have the same effect on others as the girls' lies have on Mr. Nuttel and Mrs. Sappleton?

9. What influence do stories (fiction or non-fiction) hold over our judgments? Do you think it is important to realize that stories of any kind influence our behavior? Why or why not?

VIII

A HAUNTED HOUSE

by Virginia Woolf (1914, England)

- Introduction of the Author
- Synopsis
- Text
- Words & Idioms
- Study Questions

Introduction of the Author: Virginia Woolf (1882-1941)

As one of the founders of the modernist movement and one of the most influential female authors of the twentieth century, Adeline Virginia Stephen was born in London to a family well immersed in the Arts. Her father, Sir Leslie Stephen, was a well-respected author and literary critic, and her mother was a model for Pre-Raphaelite painters.

Educated at home by her parents and given full access to her father's library, Virginia later lamented never being educated formally and losing out on all the fun physical activities busy children do. Both her father and mother were widowed and remarried. Her father had a daughter from his previous marriage, Laura, and her mother had three children from hers: Herbert, George, and Stella.

Virginia's family life was full of tragedy that took her to the edge of sanity. She would later recount how Gerald sexually abused her, and how her mother died when she was just a teenager. Stella took matrimonial duties only to die two years later. Leslie soon died slowly of a stomach cancer, and Virginia's blood brother died at the age of six. All this death caused her to succumb to a psychological breakdown.

Virginia eventually joined an elite group of writers called the Bloomsbury Group in 1899. It was established when middle class writers from Cambridge, England, including Leonard Sidney Woolf, were introduced to Virginia and her sister in Bloomsbury, central London. They met together often to discuss writing, philosophy, and art. Through their close-knit society, they extended their view of modernism.

Many within the group married each other, Virginia and Leonard included, and most writers, except E.M. Forster, found literary success rather late. Not until World War I in 1914 did the Bloomsbury view of modernism come to an end.

When Virginia was 22 years old, her father passed away, and she moved into a house with her surviving sister and two brothers. A year later she started to write professionally and submitted articles to the Times Literary Supplement, a weekly literary review paper. Her first article was about the Bronte sisters' literary residence, Haworth. Her love for literature continued throughout her life. As a type of pilgrimage, she visited Greece in 1906 with a copy of Homer's Odyssey in hand.

Her next great adventure was to marry at the age of 30 Leonard Woolf, who had become an established author in his own right. In 1912, Virginia and Leonard created as a hobby Hogarth Press, a publishing press by which they first printed titles by hand. Many of their titles included not only those of their Bloombury group but also T.S. Eliot's *The Wasteland* (1924), Sigmund Freud's works, and translations of foreign books. Virginia and Leonard, as were all of the Bloombury Group, were against World War II; Leonard was not called to fight due to a trembling in his hands, but both had agreed to kill themselves if the Nazi's ever annexed London and captured them.

Though Virginia Woolf wrote feminist writings, essays (over 500), and many short stories, readers especially remember her novels. She published her first novel, *The Voyage Out*, in 1915, followed by *Jacob's Room* (1922) and *Mrs. Dalloway* (1925). Her following two novels, *To the Lighthouse* (1927), and *The Waves* (1931), established her as one of the foremost writers of modernism, which experimented with exploring the highly private inner self and often employed the stream-of-consciousness technique. It is probably her best-known novel, *Orlando* (1928), that she receives the most recognition. Ultimately, Virginia had wanted it to be the start of a new trend of combining biography with fiction. Though the trend never caught on, it is seen as the epitome of women's literature dealing with women's issues, and even the taboo concept of lesbians, without causing any scandal. Virginia originally wrote it as a way to show her love and affection for a woman she had a lesbian affair with, the novelist/poet Vita Sackville-West, who appeared on the covers of the first editions dressed as the male Orlando.

With the advent of World War II in 1939, Virginia slipped in and out of depression. Though there was no diagnosis at the time, modern doctors have classified her sickness as bipolar disorder, which accompanies mood swings and depression. The Nazi bombing of London that lasted 57 nights and resulted in the total devastation of the city and harsh criticism surrounding her then recently published nonfiction works pushed her further into depression with no way out.

On March 28,1941, less than a month before the bombing of London ceased, Virginia Woolf filled her pockets with stones and, walking into the river near her house, committed suicide. Her body was not found until 28 days later. Her suicide note left for her husband has been analyzed and to this day has influenced how critics view her works: "I feel certain that I am going mad again. I feel we can't go through another of those terrible times. And I shan't recover this time. I begin to hear voices, and I can't concentrate. So I am doing what seems the best thing to do."[4]

4 From Virginia Woolf's suicide note

Synopsis

A female narrator wakes and hears a ghostly couple wandering through a house, opening and shutting doors. They whisper to each other looking for some "buried treasure."

The narrator can hear the ghostly couple, even sense their presence, but she cannot see them. She cannot only hear them in the morning, but she can also hear them throughout the day as well.

The narrator relaxes out in her garden, reading a book. Again, she hears the ghostly couple whispering and moving around the house in continuous search of their treasure. Thinking they have found it, she enters the house only to find it empty, all the doors open. Instead of voices, she can hear a wood pigeon at the window and the threshing machine out on the farm.

It is then that the narrator wonders why she has entered the house. She thinks she can find her answer upstairs in the loft. Again, she fails to find the ghosts. Instead, she sees ghostly reflections of apples on the window pane, green leaves fallen on the grass outside, even the shadow of a thrush moving across the carpet.

All the while, she hears the house pulsing like a beating heart with the words "safe, safe, safe." It is the buried treasure that makes this house safe.

Evening comes, the sun sets, and the house darkens. The narrator seeks solace from the light burning behind the glass of her lamp. And just as the glass is an unseen barrier between life and the flame, so is death the unseen barrier that separates the narrator and the ghosts.

The female ghost was the first of the couple to die hundreds of years ago, so, out of despair, the husband locked up the house, room by darkening room, and left to travel the world—north, east, and south. Probably having found what he was looking for, the husband returned to the house in the country, presumably where his wife was buried, and the house pulsed with the same words, "Safe, safe, safe."

Now, though a storm rages outside the house, the light inside is undisturbed, allowing the living couple to sleep in peace. The ghostly couple, however, still wander the halls, opening all the doors, looking for joy.

The ghostly couple reminisces over their good days, the kisses, walking together, sharing the winters together.

The doors shut throughout the house, echoing the pulse of the house.

The ghostly pair then enters the sleeping couple's room, looking upon the living with longing. Outside, the storm still rages. But the spirits sense the love between the husband and wife.

The ghosts ponder the sleeping couple, and the love they still hold for each other, their unseen joy. The ghosts have found their hidden treasure. It was sleeping, reading in the garden, laughing, working in the loft all this time. It was not in the house after all.

The narrator wakes, knowing what the buried treasure the ghostly couple seek: the light and love found in the heart of the living.

Text

Whatever hour you woke there was a door shutting. From room to room they went, hand in hand, lifting here, opening there, making sure—a ghostly couple.

"Here we left it," she said. And he added, "Oh, but here too!" "It's upstairs," she murmured. "And in the garden," he whispered. "Quietly," they said, "or we shall wake them."

But it wasn't that you woke us. Oh, no. "They're looking for it; they're drawing the curtain," one might say, and so read on a page or two. "Now they've found it," one would be certain, stopping the pencil on the margin. And then, tired of reading, one might rise and see for oneself, the house all empty, the doors standing open, only the wood pigeons bubbling with content and the hum of the threshing machine sounding from the farm. "What did I come in here for? What did I want to find?" My hands were empty. "Perhaps it's upstairs then?" The apples were in the loft. And so down again, the garden still as ever, only the book had slipped into the grass.

But they had found it in the drawing room. Not that one could ever see them. The window panes reflected apples, reflected roses; all the leaves were green in the glass. If they moved in the drawing room, the apple only turned its yellow side. Yet, the moment after, if the door was opened, spread about the floor, hung upon the walls, pendant from the ceiling—what? My hands were empty. The shadow of a thrush crossed the carpet; from the deepest wells of silence the wood pigeon drew its bubble of sound. "Safe, safe, safe," the pulse of the house beat softly. "The treasure buried; the room ..." the pulse stopped short. Oh, was that the buried treasure?

A moment later the light had faded. Out in the garden then? But the trees spun darkness for a wandering beam of sun. So fine, so rare, coolly sunk beneath the surface the beam I sought always burnt behind the glass. Death was the glass; death was between us; coming to the woman first, hundreds of years ago, leaving the house, sealing all the windows; the rooms were darkened. He left it, left her, went North, went East, saw the stars turned in the Southern sky; sought the house, found it dropped beneath the Downs. "Safe, safe, safe," the pulse of the house beat gladly. "The Treasure yours."

The wind roars up the avenue. Trees stoop and bend this way and that. Moonbeams splash and spill wildly in the rain. But the beam of the lamp falls straight from the window. The candle burns stiff and still. Wandering through the house, opening the win-

dows, whispering not to wake us, the ghostly couple seek their joy.

"Here we slept," she says. And he adds, "Kisses without number." "Waking in the morning—" "Silver between the trees—" "Upstairs—" "In the garden—" "When summer came—" "In winter snowtime—" The doors go shutting far in the distance, gently knocking like the pulse of a heart.

Nearer they come; cease at the doorway. The wind falls, the rain slides silver down the glass. Our eyes darken; we hear no steps beside us; we see no lady spread her ghostly cloak. His hands shield the lantern. "Look," he breathes. "Sound asleep. Love upon their lips."

Stooping, holding their silver lamp above us, long they look and deeply. Long they pause. The wind drives straightly; the flame stoops slightly. Wild beams of moonlight cross both floor and wall, and, meeting, stain the faces bent; the faces pondering; the faces that search the sleepers and seek their hidden joy.

"Safe, safe, safe," the heart of the house beats proudly. "Long years—" he sighs. "Again you found me." "Here," she murmurs, "sleeping; in the garden reading; laughing, rolling apples in the loft. Here we left our treasure—" Stooping, their light lifts the lids upon my eyes. "Safe! safe! safe!" the pulse of the house beats wildly. Waking, I cry "Oh, is this *your* buried treasure? The light in the heart."

Words & Idioms

bubble: (v) to sing in a cheerful manner
downs: (n) an area with grassy hills
drawing room: (n phr) reception room
moon beam: (n phr) moon light, usually reflected on floating dust.
pendant: (n) an ornament that hangs from the ceiling
Southern Sky: (n phr) the southern hemisphere
thrush: (n) a songbird
Trees spun darkness: (idiom) trees cast shadows

Study Questions

1. Are the ghosts in the story real? Or are they simply a figment of the narrator's imagination? Give details from the story to support your opinion.

2. Because of the ending, this can be considered a love story. Is it? If so, then why is there no mention of the spouse? The narrator only gives plural pronouns to indicate a spouse. What is the reason for this?

3. Readers assume that the narrator is a woman, but it could easily be a man. What do you think? Explain your answer with evidence from the story.

4. Is this a ghost story, or a love story? Explain your answer with evidence from the story.

5. This story is what is now called flash fiction. What is flash fiction? And how does it fit into that category?

6. Does this story have a plot? Can it be considered a story? Or is it more of a free verse poem? Use evidence from the story to support your answer.

7. “A Haunted House” was published in 1921, the same year Woolf published an essay on Henry James’s ghost stories. In it, she challenged new writers to give a modernist take on the classic form of ghost stories:

> To admit that the supernatural was used for the last time by Mrs. Radcliffe and that modern nerves are immune from the wonder and terror which ghosts have always inspired would be to throw up the sponge too easily. If the old methods are obsolete, it is the business of a writer to discover new ones. The public can feel again what it has once felt—there can be no doubt about that; only from time to time the point of attack must be changed.[5]

8. Do you think this story fits Woolf’s criteria above? How? Does this story give wonder and terror to the reader? Explain with evidence from the story.

9. In what ways is this a modernist ghost story? How does it differ from the classic versions? How is it the same?

5 *Times Literary Supplement*, December 22, 1921.

Continental Short Stories

Guy De Maupassant: The Diamond Necklace (1884)

Leo Tolstoy: Three Questions (1885)

IX

THE DIAMOND NECKLACE

by Guy de Maupassant (1884, France)

- Introduction of the Author
- Synopsis
- Text
- Words & Idioms
- Study Questions

Introduction of the Author: Guy De Maupassant (1850-1893)

Considered the greatest French short story writer, Guy De Maupassant is most famous for his naturalistic style of writing and as the father of the modern short story. Maupassant was born of affluent parents, and when his mother was in her youth, she was even playmates with Gustave Flaubert (1821-1880), who later became most famous for his novel *Madame Bovary* (1857). His mother had great literary tastes, and having known the great Flaubert, Maupassant chose to stay with his mother when his parents divorced. In his late teens, he even had the opportunity to meet Flaubert, who later became his mentor and had a great influence on his writing.

Maupassant continued his schooling, and though he may have had a rebellious streak, he aimed to become a scholar, showing greater interest in poetry and theater. However, with the breakout of the Franco-Prussian war (1870-1871), he volunteered to fight for his country, yet his rebellious streak continued, and the army was forced to discipline him on several occasions. Upon the end of the war, when France lost most of its empire, Maupassant settled in Paris where he worked as a clerk for the Navy. There, he may have dwindled into obscurity if not for his literary hero, Flaubert.

Making him his protege, Flaubert helped Maupassant break into journalism and even invited him into his literary circle that included the likes of Henry James and Emile Zola. By 1880, Maupassant had Published his first short story that is arguably his best, "*Boule de Souif*," which takes place during the Franco-Prussian war. *Boule de Souif*, literally translated as "Ball of Fat," is the name of a nationalistic prostitute who flees with nine other refugees by stage coach from their town now occupied by the Prussians. He used the story to contrast the amorality of the middle class with the patriotism of a lower-class prostitute. This story was one of many in a collected volume, and with its success, he followed his acclaim by writing prolifically three to four volumes of short stories a year. In a ten-year period, he had written around 300 short stories.

At the same time, he even wrote six novels, his first being *A Woman's Life* (*Une Vie*, 1883). Though his writing was popular, Maupassant avoided society life and took great joy in voyaging around Europe and Africa in his private yacht. After each trip, he would have a new volume of stories to sell.

Maupassant's stories have been labeled naturalistic in that they imitate or represent what is real as opposed to romantic stories that stress the fanciful or unreal. The naturalistic school, which Flaubert championed at its early stages and Maupassant reveled in, started in France as a direct reaction to the Romantic Movement.

Realist literature centers on the middle class by depicting events and their consequences with as little bias on the writer's part as possible. A good example is "The Diamond Necklace," which has a middle-class couple suffer the indignity of having to scrounge and save to pay for a borrowed jewel necklace they have lost, only to find out that the necklace was a worthless fake. Such social issues as social equality, justice, unemployment, and poverty play important roles in the naturalistic school, where "The Diamond Necklace" emphasizes overreaching one's goals for superficial ideals.

Even his thirty-nine horror stories, though closely resembling Edgar Allan Poe's style of romantic psychological horror, detail the downward spiral of the protagonists into madness that was often the result of a troubled mind more than outside forces. With such range to his stories, Maupassant's horror fiction has influenced many writers, including horror writer H.P. Lovecraft, master story teller O. Henry, who uses a similar style with twist endings, and playwright Anton Chekhov.

Maupassant's idea of the modern novel was not to aim at "telling a story or entertaining us or touching our hearts but at forcing us to think and understand the deeper, hidden meaning of events." This statement takes on a rather ironic twist, as his stories are want to do, when he wrote a rather effective horror short story called "*Le Horla*" (1887). *Le Horla* (from French "*Hors*," outside, and "*de la*," there) are strange beings that cannot be seen and are cousins to the vampire, but the narrator senses one of them coming off of a ghost ship. It eventually drives him mad, and he commits suicide to rid himself of it.

In the early 1870's, Maupassant had contracted syphilis, which causes mental disorders. As his dementia grew worse so did his paranoia of persecution. Many critics feel that "*Le Horla*" was written under the sickness of dementia and has a type of autobiographical sensibility to it. His never-ending quest for isolation from fame led him to ultimately slit his own throat. He was committed to an asylum where he eventually died on July 6, 1893, six years after writing "*Le Horla*."

Synopsis

Mathilde is a beautiful and charming woman born to middle-class parents. As was the custom of her time, it was difficult to marry a man in a higher class, so she marries a poor clerk, who has the same profession as her father.

She always feels she is destined for a better life in the upper class since she was born with natural beauty and an understanding of fashion and style. However, she lacks the money and means to dress in the latest fashions or furnish her house in the luxuries befitting her heart. Even the meals they eat are never to her satisfaction.

One evening her husband returns home with an invitation to the palace of the Ministry. Instead of being glad, she is furious since all of the upper-class society will be in attendance. Her husband cannot understand her disappointment. She has nothing to wear either for clothes or jewelry. So, she declines the invitation.

He asks her how much she needs to buy a new dress and she says two thousand dollars. He has the money but had already planned on buying a gun and going on a hunting trip. But in the end, he agrees to buy her the dress.

The week of the party, Mathilde is still depressed. She has the dress but no jewelry to wear with it. So, again, she refuses to go. He wishes she would wear flowers as decoration, but only the poor wear such. He suddenly remembers her rich friend, Mrs. Forestier. She could go and borrow some jewelry from her. She agrees and does just that.

Mrs. Forestier opens a box of jewel necklaces and bracelets for Mathilde to choose from. She keeps trying on more and more since she can't make up her mind until she comes upon a wondrous diamond necklace in a black satin box. Her friend then lends it to her.

During the magnificent party, Mathilde feels rich and happy. She feels that she truly belongs in the upper class. She dances, chats with all the ladies, and has an exquisite time. By 4 am., she finally goes home with her husband, exhausted but happy.

When they arrive home, Mathilde notices the diamond necklace is missing! She remembers having it before getting in the cab, so she must have lost it in the carriage. Her husband goes and looks for it but does not find it. He decides to tell Mrs. Forestier that the clasp had broken and they would need to fix it before returning it.

After a week of searching, she realizes it is lost. They will need to buy a new one as a replacement. After searching many jewelers for a necklace that look similar to the one they lost, they finally find one, at close to $100,000.00.

The husband has saved some money, about half the price, and they will try to borrow the rest. He borrows all the money they need, but it will take the rest of his life to pay it all back.

Mathilde takes the new necklace to Mrs. Forestier, who accepts it without even looking at it. Meanwhile, the couple has to sell their house for a rented room and dismiss their only servant. Mathilde even has to find employment by working several dirty jobs. Her husband has to get a second job just to pay back all their debt. They live their life in destitute, worse off than Mathilde has ever known. Her natural beauty fades, and she ages more than her years.

She misses her old life of plenty.

One Sunday while out on a walk, Mathilde runs into Mrs. Forestier, who fails to recognize the aged Mathilde. She feels she must confess what happened to the diamond necklace and tells her acquaintance all her hardship over that one mistake. She is surprised that Mrs. Forestier has never noticed the swap.

Mrs. Forestier then admits that her original diamond necklace was a fake, costing only 2,500 dollars!

Text

She was one of those pretty and charming girls who are sometimes, as if by a mistake of destiny, born in a family of clerks. She had no dowry, no expectations, no means of being known, understood, loved, wedded, by any rich and distinguished man; and she let herself be married to a little clerk at the Ministry of Public Instruction.

She dressed plainly because she could not dress well, but she was as unhappy as though she had really fallen from her proper station; since with women there is neither caste nor rank; and beauty, grace, and charm act instead of family and birth. Natural fineness, instinct for what is elegant, suppleness of wit, are the sole hierarchy, and make from women of the people the equals of the very greatest ladies.

She suffered ceaselessly, feeling herself born for all the delicacies and all the luxuries. She suffered from the poverty of her dwelling, from the wretched look of the walls, from the worn-out chairs, from the ugliness of the curtains. All those things, of which another woman of her rank would never even have been conscious, tortured her and made her angry.

The sight of the little Breton peasant who did her humble housework aroused in her regrets which were despairing, and distracted dreams. She thought of the silent ante-chambers hung with Oriental tapestry, lit by tall bronze candelabra, and of the two great footmen in knee-breeches who sleep in the big arm-chairs, made drowsy by the heavy warmth of the hot-air stove. She thought

of the long *salons* fitted up with ancient silk, of the delicate furniture carrying priceless curiosities, and of the coquettish perfumed boudoirs made for talks at five o'clock with intimate friends, with men famous and sought after, whom all women envy and whose attention they all desire.

When she sat down to dinner, before the round table covered with a tablecloth three days old, opposite her husband, who uncovered the soup-tureen and declared with an enchanted air, "Ah, the good *pot-au-feu!* I don't know anything better than that," she thought of dainty dinners, of shining silverware, of tapestry which peopled the walls with ancient personages and with strange birds flying in the midst of a fairy forest; and she thought of delicious dishes served on marvellous plates, and of the whispered gallantries which you listen to with a sphinx-like smile, while you are eating the pink flesh of a trout or the wings of a quail.

She had no dresses, no jewels, nothing. And she loved nothing but that; she felt made for that. She would so have liked to please, to be envied, to be charming, to be sought after.

She had a friend, a former schoolmate at the convent, who was rich, and whom she did not like to go and see any more, because she suffered so much when she came back.

But, one evening, her husband returned home with a triumphant air, and holding a large envelope in his hand.

"There," said he, "here is something for you."

She tore the paper sharply, and drew out a printed card which bore these words:

"The Minister of Public Instruction and Mme. Georges

Ramponneau request the honor of M. and Mme. Loisel's company at the palace of the Ministry on Monday evening, January 18th."

Instead of being delighted, as her husband hoped, she threw the invitation on the table with disdain, murmuring:

"What do you want me to do with that?"

"But, my dear, I thought you would be glad. You never go out, and this is such a fine opportunity. I had awful trouble to get it. Every one wants to go; it is very select, and they are not giving many invitations to clerks. The whole official world will be there."

She looked at him with an irritated eye, and she said, impatiently:

"And what do you want me to put on my back?"

He had not thought of that; he stammered:

"Why, the dress you go to the theatre in. It looks very well, to me."

He stopped, distracted, seeing that his wife was crying. Two great tears descended slowly from the corners of her eyes towards the corners of her mouth. He stuttered:

"What's the matter? What's the matter?"

But, by a violent effort, she had conquered her grief, and she replied, with a calm voice, while she wiped her wet cheeks:

"Nothing. Only I have no dress, and therefore I can't go to this ball. Give your card to some colleague whose wife is better equipped than I."

He was in despair. He resumed:

"Come, let us see, Mathilde. How much would it cost, a suitable dress, which you could use on other occasions, something very simple?"

She reflected several seconds, making her calculations and wondering also what sum she could ask without drawing on herself an immediate refusal and a frightened exclamation from the economical clerk.

Finally, she replied, hesitatingly:

"I don't know exactly, but I think I could manage it with four hundred francs."

He had grown a little pale, because he was laying aside just that amount to buy a gun and treat himself to a little shooting next summer on the plain of Nanterre, with several friends who went to shoot larks down there, of a Sunday.

But he said:

"All right. I will give you four hundred francs. And try to have a pretty dress."

###

The day of the ball drew near, and Mme. Loisel seemed sad, uneasy, anxious. Her dress was ready, however. Her husband said to her one evening:

"What is the matter? Come, you've been so queer these last three days,"

And she answered:

"It annoys me not to have a single jewel, not a single stone, nothing to put on. I shall look like distress. I should almost rather not go at all"

He resumed:

"You might wear natural flowers. It's very stylish at this time of the year. For ten francs you can get two or three magnificent roses."

She was not convinced.

"No; there's nothing more humiliating than to look poor among other women who are rich."

But her husband cried:

"How stupid you are! Go look up your friend Mme. Forestier, and ask her to lend you some jewels. You're quite

thick enough with her to do that."

She uttered a cry of joy:

"It's true. I never thought of it."

The next day she went to her friend and told of her distress.

Mme. Forestier went to a wardrobe with a glass door, took out a large jewel-box, brought it back, opened it, and said to Mme. Loisel:

"Choose, my dear."

She saw first of all some bracelets, then a pearl necklace, then a Venetian cross, gold, and precious stones of admirable workmanship. She tried on the ornaments before the glass, hesitated, could not make up her mind to part with them, to give them back. She kept asking:

"Haven't you any more?"

"Why, yes. Look. I don't know what you like."

All of a sudden she discovered, in a black satin box, a superb necklace of diamonds; and her heart began to beat with an immoderate desire. Her hands trembled as she took it. She fastened it around her throat, outside her high-necked dress, and remained lost in ecstasy at the sight of herself.

Then she asked, hesitating, filled with anguish:

"Can you lend me that, only that?"

"Why, yes, certainly."

She sprang upon the neck

of her friend, kissed her passionately, then fled with her treasure.

###

The day of the ball arrived. Mme. Loisel made a great success. She was prettier than them all, elegant, gracious, smiling, and crazy with joy. All the men looked at her, asked her name, endeavored to be introduced. All the attaches of the Cabinet wanted to waltz with her. She was remarked by the minister himself.

She danced with intoxication, with passion, made drunk by pleasure, forgetting all, in the triumph of her beauty, in the glory of her success, in a sort of cloud of happiness composed of all this homage, of all this admiration, of all these awakened desires, and of that sense of complete victory which is so sweet to woman's heart.

She went away about four o'clock in the morning. Her husband had been sleeping since mid-night, in a little deserted anteroom, with three other gentlemen whose wives were having a very good time.

He threw over her shoulders the wraps which he had brought, modest wraps of common life, whose poverty contrasted with the elegance of the ball dress. She felt this and wanted to escape so as not to be remarked by the other women, who were enveloping themselves in costly furs.

Loisel held her back.

"Wait a bit. You will catch cold outside. I will go and call a cab."

But she did not listen to him, and rapidly descended the stairs. When they were in the street they did not find a carriage; and they began to look for one, shouting after the cabmen whom they saw passing by at a distance.

They went down towards the Seine; in despair, shivering with cold. At last they found on the quay one of those an-

cient noctambulant coupés which, exactly as if they were ashamed to show their misery during the day, are never seen round Paris until after nightfall.

It took them to their door in the Rue des Martyrs, and once more, sadly, they climbed up homeward. All was ended, for her. And as to him, he reflected that he must be at the Ministry at ten o'clock.

She removed the wraps, which covered her shoulders, before the glass, so as once more to see herself in all her glory. But suddenly she uttered a cry. She had no longer the necklace around her neck!

Her husband, already half-undressed, demanded:

"What is the matter with you?"

She turned madly towards him:

"I have—I have—I've lost Mme. Forestier's necklace."

He stood up, distracted.

"What!—how?—Impossible!"

And they looked in the folds of her dress, in the folds of her cloak, in her pockets, everywhere. They did not find it.

He asked:

"You 're sure you had it on when you left the ball?"

"Yes, I felt it in the vestibule of the palace."

"But if you had lost it in the street we should have heard it fall. It must be in the cab."

"Yes. Probably. Did you take his number?"

"No. And you, didn't you notice it?"

"No."

They looked, thunderstruck, at one another. At last Loisel put on his clothes.

"I shall go back on foot," said he, "over the whole route which we have taken, to see if I can't find it."

And he went out. She sat waiting on a chair in her ball dress, without strength to go to bed, overwhelmed, without fire, without a thought.

Her husband came back about seven o'clock. He had found nothing.

He went to Police Headquarters, to the newspaper offices, to offer a reward; he went to the cab companies—everywhere, in fact, whither he was urged by the least suspicion of hope.

She waited all day, in the same condition of mad fear before this terrible calamity.

Loisel returned at night with a hollow, pale face; he had discovered nothing.

"You must write to your friend," said he, "that you have broken the clasp of her necklace and that you are having it mended. That will give us time to turn round."

She wrote at his dictation.

###

At the end of a week they had lost all hope.

And Loisel, who had aged five years, declared:

"We must consider how to replace that ornament."

The next day they took the box which had contained it, and they went to the jeweller whose name was found within. He consulted his books.

"It was not I, madame, who sold that necklace; I must simply have furnished the case."

Then they went from jeweller to jeweller, searching for a

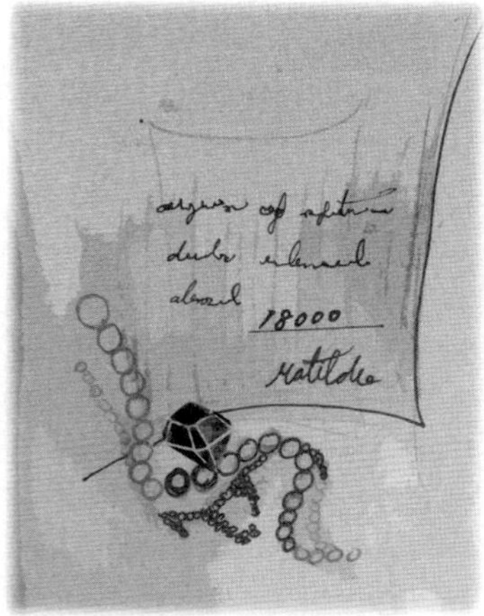

necklace like the other, consulting their memories, sick both of them with chagrin and with anguish.

They found, in a shop at the Palais Royal, a string of diamonds which seemed to them exactly like the one they looked for. It was worth forty thousand francs. They could have it for thirty-six.

So they begged the jeweller not to sell it for three days yet. And they made a bargain that he should buy it back for thirty-four thousand francs, in case they found the other one before the end of February.

Loisel possessed eighteen thousand francs which his father had left him. He would borrow the rest.

He did borrow, asking a thousand francs of one, five hundred of another, five louis here, three louis there. He gave notes, took up ruinous obligations, dealt with usurers, and all the race of lenders. He compromised all the rest of his life, risked his signature without even knowing if he could meet it; and, frightened by the pains yet to come, by the black misery which was about to fall upon him, by the prospect of all the physical privations and of all the moral tortures which he was to suffer, he went to get the new necklace, putting down upon the merchant's counter thirty-six thousand francs.

When Mme. Loisel took back the necklace Mme. Forestier said to her, with a chilly manner:

"You should have returned it sooner, I might have needed it."

She did not open the case, as her friend had so much feared. If she had detected the substitution, what would she have thought, what would she have said? Would she not have taken Mme. Loisel for a thief?

Mme. Loisel now knew the horrible existence of the needy. She took her part, moreover, all on a sudden, with heroism. That dreadful debt must be paid. She would pay it. They dismissed their servant; they changed their lodgings; they rented a garret under the roof.

She came to know what heavy house-work meant and the odious cares of the kitchen. She washed the dishes, using her rosy nails on the greasy pots and pans. She washed the dirty linen, the shirts, and the dish-cloths, which she dried upon a line; she carried the slops down to the street every morning, and carried up the water, stopping for breath at every landing. And, dressed like a woman of the people, she went to the fruiterer, the grocer, the butcher, her basket on her arm, bargaining, insulted, defending her miserable money sou by sou.

Each month they had to meet some notes, renew others, obtain more time.

Her husband worked in the evening making a fair copy of some tradesman's accounts, and late at night he often copied manuscript for five sous a page.

And this life lasted ten years.

At the end or ten years they had paid everything, everything, with the rates of usury, and the accumulations of the compound interest.

Mme. Loisel looked old now. She had become the woman

of impoverished households—strong and hard and rough. With frowsy hair, skirts askew, and red hands, she talked loud while washing the floor with great swishes of water. But sometimes, when her husband was at the office, she sat down near the window, and she thought of that gay evening of long ago, of that ball where she had been so beautiful and so feted.

What would have happened if she had not lost that necklace? Who knows? who knows? How life is strange and changeful! How little a thing is needed for us to be lost or to be saved!

###

But, one Sunday, having gone to take a walk in the Champs Elysées to refresh herself from the labors of the week, she suddenly perceived a woman who was leading a child. It was Mme. Forestier, still young, still beautiful, still charming.

Mme. Loisel felt moved. Was she going to speak to her? Yes, certainly. And now that she had paid, she was going to tell her all about it. Why not?

She went up.

"Good-day, Jeanne."

The other, astonished to be familiarly addressed by this plain goodwife, did not recognize her at all, and stammered:

"But—madame!—I do not know—You must have mistaken."

"No. I am Mathilde Loisel."

Her friend uttered a cry.

"Oh, my poor Mathilde! How you are changed!"

"Yes, I have had days hard enough, since I have seen you, days wretched enough—and that because of you!"

"Of me! How so?"

"Do you remember that diamond necklace which you lent me to wear at the ministerial ball?"

"Yes. Well?"

"Well, I lost it."

"What do you mean? You brought it back."

"I brought you back another just like it. And for this we have been ten years paying. You can understand that it was not easy for us, us who had nothing. At last it is ended, and I am very glad."

Mme. Forestier had stopped.

"You say that you bought a necklace of diamonds to replace mine?"

"Yes. You never noticed it, then! They were very like."

And she smiled with a joy which was proud and naive at once.

Mme. Forestier, strongly moved, took her two hands.

"Oh, my poor Mathilde! Why, my necklace was paste. It was worth at most five hundred francs!"

Words & Idioms

10 francs: inflation and exchange adjusted to be about $51.81 (a rough estimate of what the 19th-century franc was worth compared to the 19th-century dollar: .193 French francs = 1 American dollar

18,000 francs: $93,264.80

34,000 francs: $176,165.80

40,000 francs: $207,253.89

400 francs: $2,072.54

500 francs: $2,590.50

attaché: (n) a person attached to the legislature or embassy

Breton: (n) a person from Brittany, a peninsula on the northwest tip of France

chagrin: (n) disappointment

Champs Elysees: (n) a prestigious street in Paris with many cafes and theaters

coquettish: (adj) flirtatious

dowry: (n) money the bride's family saves to give to the groom's family

homage: (n) respect given

immoderate: (adj) excessive

ingenuity: (adj) imagination

lark: (n) a small singing bird, popular for shooting as sport

Louis: (n) a coin similar in value to the franc; introduced by Louis XIII in 1640 that bore his likeness (replaced again in 1795 by the franc)

Nanterre: (n) a commune in northern France, now a western suburb of Paris

odious: (adj) detestable

Palais Royal: an old palace and garden area that, in Maupassant's time, had a popular boulevard of cafes and theaters; currently located across the street from the Louvre
paste: (n) artificial gem made of glass
privation: (n) comfort
quail: (n) a small game bird whose meat was as popular as chicken
quay: (n) a landing place for boats; a wharf
Queer: (adj) strange or odd
Rue des Matyrs: (translated: Street of Martyrs) a street located in northern Paris
Seine: (n) a river that flows northwest through Paris and drains into the English Channel
sou: (n) bronze coin of France; similar in value to a penny
sphinx-like: (adj) mysterious
supple: (adj) flexible
Tureen: (n) a large, deep bowl used for serving soup
usurer: (n) a person who lends money with a large amount of interest; loan shark (modern usage)
vestibule: (n) an antechamber between the door and the interior of the house

Study Questions

1. After all Mathilde has suffered through, do you think she is redeemed by the revelation at the end of the story, making this a happy ending? Or is she to continue in poverty with the knowledge that she has foolishly condemned her family to this state, making this a tragic ending?

2. Will Madame Forestier return the real necklace for compensation over the lost fake one?

3. If Madame Forestier does give the necklace back, will Mathilde have learned her lesson and save the money, or will she spend it all on what she wants, as she would have at the beginning of the story?

4. What would you have done in the same situation at the end of the story if you were Madame Forestier?

5. What is your opinion of Mathilde? What kind of person is she?

6. What defines the true character of Mathilde: honesty, humility, and hardworking, or the clothes and jewels that she seeks to wear?

7. If you understand how men treated women in the nineteenth century, can you blame Mathilde for her actions? What other options would she have to fulfill her sense of self-worth as a woman in a male society?

8. What is your opinion of Loisel? What kind of person is he?

9. Is Mathilde an unfortunate victim of fate (determinism), or is she a victim of her own bad choices that she has made (free will)? Use details from the text to support your answer.

10. The men at the ball treated Mathilde as a princess. How would they have treated her if they knew her necklace was a fake and she was middle-class?

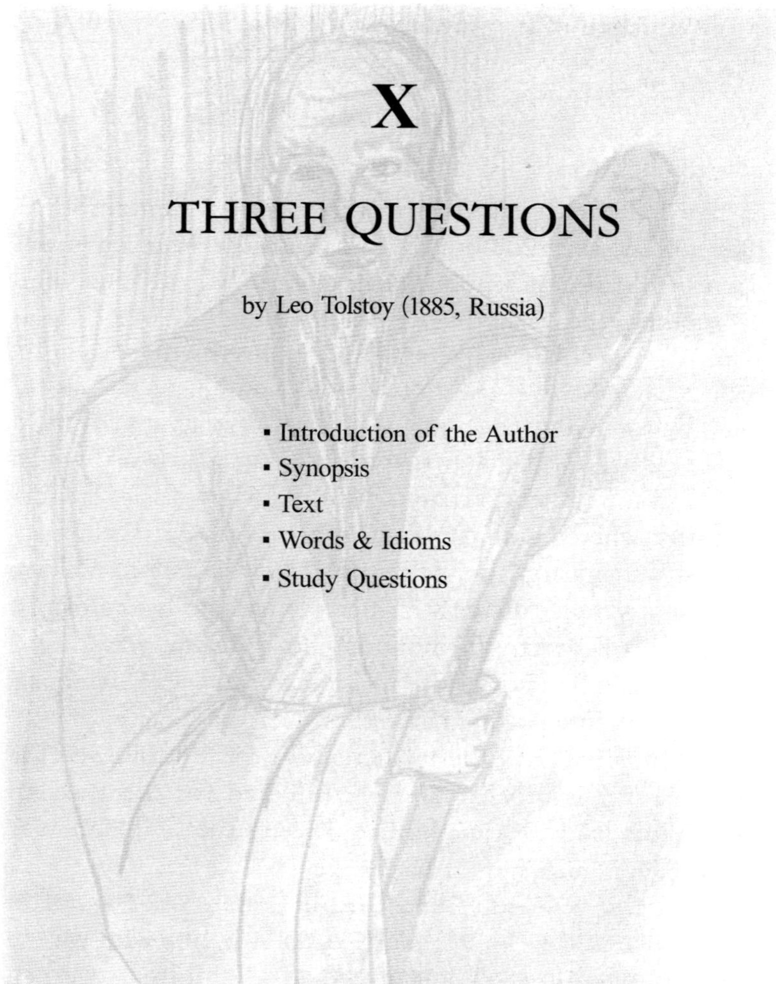

X

THREE QUESTIONS

by Leo Tolstoy (1885, Russia)

- Introduction of the Author
- Synopsis
- Text
- Words & Idioms
- Study Questions

Introduction of the Author: Leo Tolstoy (1828-1910)

Lev Nikolayevich Tolstoy was born on September 9, 1828, on an estate 200 km south of Moscow, Russia. He was born of old Russian nobility; his father was a Count and his mother a princess; thus, he received the title of Count as well. When his parents passed away, he lived with several female relatives over the duration of his youth, and he was tutored by foreign teachers mainly from Germany and France.

He studied Oriental languages at Kazan University, which he found too difficult, so he transferred to the easier law department where he underwhelmed his professors. Feeling academia was not for him, he returned to his estate to manage and live a simpler life as a farmer. He tried to use reformist ideals with his serfs (farmhands), but since he was always absent enjoying a social life in Moscow and St. Petersburg, his farm became poorly managed.

Not satisfied with the farmer's life, Tolstoy followed the example of his brother and volunteered for the Russian army. This lead to him fighting during the Crimean War from 1854 to 1855.

After the war, he returned to his estate once again to settle down and write. He married Sofia Behrs, who was 16 years younger, in 1862, and they had 13 children together, with three dying in their infancy. With her full support—she acted as his secretary, editor, and financial manager—he was able to compose his two greatest works, *War and Peace* (1873) and *Anna Karenina* (published in installments from 1873-1877). The English editions were published under the name Leo Tolstoy.

Tolstoy was a prolific writer, where he wrote essays and philosophical tracts on the meaning of life and the nature of good and evil. He also became interested in education. He founded thirteen schools to apply his ideas of democratic education practically. However, due to pressure from the Tsar's secret police, Tolstoy's schools did not last long.

Near the turn of the century, Tolstoy's beliefs and writing began to take a more radical philosophy. Finding no peace in the Russian Orthodox Church, he decided to develop his own beliefs and published several tracts on this philosophy. He once wrote:

> **I put men to death in war, I fought duels to slay others. I lost at cards, wasted the substance wrung from the sweat of peasants, punished the latter cruelly, rioted with loose women, and deceived men. Lying, robbery, adultery of all kinds, drunkenness, violence, and murder, all were committed by me, not one crime omitted, and yet I was not the less considered by my equals to be a comparatively moral man. Such was my life for ten years[6].**

He increasingly found his life of wealth and fame empty and wanted to give away his money, which caused a rift in the relationship with his wife. To appease her, he signed over all his copyrights and royalties before 1881 to her name.

For the next 29 years, Tolstoy created a worldwide following as a religious and moral writer. Fans and followers of Tolstoy's writings would show up at his home for discussions. The radical ideas they discussed would distress his wife even more and set their marriage problems into the public sector.

---

6 Tolstoy, Leo. *My Confession.*

In his search to find God, he secretly left his estate to his daughter, Alexandria, and his doctor, on some pilgrimage, free of his wife and the press. Days later, proving to be too old for travel at the age of 82, Tolstoy had to stop at a tiny railroad station to rest. Staying with the station master to recover, he shortly died there on November 20, 1910.

Synopsis

A certain king decides he wants to find the key to success. He offers his subjects a great reward if one can answer his three questions.

The first question he asks is how he can learn to do the right action at the right time. The answers vary from having a set schedule to never being idle. Others offer that a council should be available to offer their wisdom while others suggest magicians to foretell all significant events because councils take too long.

The second question the King asks is who the King should listen to in order to be successful. The answers to this question are just as varied, with the answers given by councilors, priests, and doctors—even warriors.

The King's third question is how he would know what the most important task would be. Again, the answers vary from science to skill in war, and even religious worship.

Since the answers vary and are so different, the King rejects all of them so no one can collect the reward. Instead, he decides to ask a wise hermit the three questions.

To meet the hermit out in the forest, the King dresses in simple clothes. The weak hermit is digging near his hut. The king then asks his three questions. The hermit doesn't respond and only continues his digging.

The King offers to dig to give the hermit time to rest and think. After much work and asking of his questions, night has approached, and still, the Hermit has not offered any answer.

Just then, a bearded man comes running out of the forest. He is wounded in the stomach and faints at the King's feet. It is such a deadly wound that the King has trouble stopping the bleeding. Only after much toil does he get the injured man bandaged. He then fetches some water for the man and carries him into the Hermit's hut to rest. The King, being exhausted from his labors, falls asleep at the door.

Upon waking, the King sees the man staring at him. The man apologizes and asks for forgiveness. The King does not understand. The man explains that he has hated the King since his brother's execution and all his property was taken. Knowing the King would be alone, the man decided to kill the King when he left the Hermit's house.

However, when the King did not return, he went to the Hermit's house and was attacked by the body guards. Escaping, he would have died, if the King had not taken mercy and healed him.

In exchange, the man offers himself and his children to be the King's slaves. The King is relieved that an enemy was so easily turned into a friend. He offers the man a doctor for his healing, servants to attend him, and restoration of his lands.

Leaving the hut, the King once again looks for the Hermit to ask one final time his three questions. He finds him out in the field planting seeds in the earth that the King had dug up the day before. The Hermit tells him that the question had already been answered.

The most important time was when the King was digging because this delayed his leaving and saved his life. On the other hand, when the wounded man arrived, the most important time was healing him, for he would have died otherwise. Therefore, the most important time is now because it is the only time that can be controlled.

Likewise, the most important man was the Hermit because he was someone to help. However, the wounded man was also the most important later that evening because the

King was able to heal his body as well as his hate. Thus, the most important people are those who are in each other's company, for there is no one else to deal with at that time.

Finally, the most important task was helping the Hermit. Later that night, healing the wounded man became the most important task because there is nothing more important at the moment than doing good to whomever one is with.

Text

It once occurred to a certain king that if he always knew the right time to begin everything; if he knew who were the right people to listen to, and whom to avoid; and, above all, if he always knew what was the most important thing to do, he would never fail in anything he might undertake.

And this thought having occurred to him, he had it proclaimed throughout his kingdom that he would give a great reward to anyone who would teach him what was the right time for every action, and who were the most necessary people, and how he might know what was the most important thing to do.

And learned men came to the king, but they all answered his questions differently.

In reply to the first question, some said that to know the right time for every action, one must draw up in advance a table of days, months, and years, and must live strictly according to it. Only thus, said they, could everything be done at its proper time. Others declared that it was impossible to decide beforehand the right time for every action, but that, not letting oneself be absorbed in idle pastimes, one should always attend to all that was going on, and then do what was most needful. Others, again, said that however attentive the king might be to what was going on, it was impossible for one man to decide correctly the right time for every action, but that he should have a council of wise men who would help him to fix the proper time for everything.

But then again others said there were some things which could not wait to be laid before a council, but about which one had at once to decide whether to undertake them or not. But in order to decide that, one must know beforehand what was going to happen. It is only magicians who know that; and, therefore, in order to know the right time for every action, one must consult magicians.

Equally various were the answers to the second question. Some said the people the king most needed were his councilors; others, the priests; others, the doctors; while some said the warriors were the most necessary.

To the third question, as to what was the most important occupation, some replied that the most important thing in the world was science. Others said it was skill in warfare; and others, again, that it was religious worship.

All the answers being different, the king agreed with none of them, and gave the reward to none. But still wishing to find the right answers to his questions, he decided to consult a hermit, widely renowned for his wisdom.

The hermit lived in a wood which he never quitted, and he received none but common folk. So the king put on simple clothes and, before reaching the hermit's cell, dismounted from his horse. Leaving his bodyguard behind, he went on alone.

When the king approached, the hermit was digging the ground in front of his hut. Seeing the king, he greeted him and went on digging. The hermit was frail and weak, and each time he stuck his spade into the ground and turned a little earth, he breathed heavily.

The king went up to him and said: "I have come to you, wise hermit, to ask you to answer three questions: How can I learn to do the right thing at the right time? Who are the people I most need, and to whom should I, therefore, pay more attention than to the rest? And, what affairs are the most important and need my first attention?"

The hermit listened to the king, but answered nothing. He just spat on his hand and recommenced digging.

"You are tired," said the king, "let me take the spade and work awhile for you."

"Thanks!" said the hermit, and, giving the spade to the king, he sat down on the ground.

When he had dug two beds, the king stopped and repeated his questions. The hermit again gave no answer, but rose, stretched out his hand for the spade, and said:

"Now rest awhile – and let me work a bit."

But the king did not give him the spade, and continued to dig. One hour passed, and another. The sun began to sink behind the trees, and the king at last stuck the spade into the ground, and said:

"I came to you, wise man, for an answer to my questions. If you can give me none, tell me so, and I will return home."

"Here comes someone running," said the hermit. "Let us see who it is."

The king turned round and saw a bearded man come running out of the wood. The man held his hands pressed

against his stomach, and blood was flowing from under them. When he reached the king, he fell fainting on the ground, moaning feebly. The king and the hermit unfastened the man's clothing. There was a large wound in his stomach. The king washed it as best he could, and bandaged it with his handkerchief and with a towel the hermit had. But the blood would not stop flowing, and the king again and again removed the bandage soaked with warm blood, and washed and re-bandaged the wound. When at last the blood ceased flowing, the man revived and asked for something to drink. The king brought fresh water and gave it to him. Meanwhile the sun had set, and it had become cool. So the king, with the hermit's help, carried the wounded man into the hut and laid him on the bed. Lying on the bed, the man closed his eyes and was quiet; but the king was so tired from his walk and from the work he had done that he crouched down on the threshold, and also fell asleep – so soundly that he slept all through the short summer night.

When he awoke in the morning, it was long before he could remember where he was, or who was the strange bearded man lying on the bed and gazing intently at him with shining eyes.

"Forgive me!" said the bearded man in a weak voice, when he saw that the king was awake and was looking at him.

"I do not know you, and have nothing to forgive you

for," said the king.

"You do not know me, but I know you. I am that enemy of yours who swore to revenge himself on you, because you executed his brother and seized his property. I knew you had gone alone to see the hermit, and I resolved to kill you on your way back. But the day passed and you did not return. So I came out from my ambush to find you, and came upon your bodyguard, and they recognized me, and wounded me. I escaped from them, but should have bled to death had you not dressed my wound. I wished to kill you, and you have saved my life. Now, if I live, and if you wish it, I will serve you as your most faithful slave, and will bid my sons do the same. Forgive me!"

The king was very glad to have made peace with his enemy so easily, and to have gained him for a friend, and he not only forgave him, but said he would send his servants and his own physician to attend him, and promised to restore his property.

Having taken leave of the wounded man, the king went out into the porch and looked around for the hermit. Before going away he wished once more to beg an answer to the questions he had put. The hermit was outside, on his knees, sowing seeds in the beds that had been dug the day before.

The king approached him and said, "For the last time, I pray you to answer my questions, wise man."

"You have already been answered!" said the hermit, still crouching on his thin legs, and looking up at the king, who stood before him.

"How answered? What do you mean?" asked the king.

"Do you not see?" replied the hermit. "If you had not pitied my weakness yesterday, and had not dug these beds for me, but had gone your way, that man would have attacked you, and you would have repented of not having stayed with me. So the most important time was when you were digging the beds; and I was the most important man; and to do me good was your most important business. Afterwards, when that man ran to us, the most important time was when you were attending to him, for if you had not bound up his wounds he would have died without having made peace with you. So he was the most important man, and what you did for him was your most important business. Remember then: there is only one time that is important – now! It is the most important time because it is the only time when we have any power. The most necessary person is the one with whom you are, for no man knows whether he will ever have dealings with anyone else: and the most important affair is to do that person good, because for that purpose alone was man sent into this life."[7]

7 Translated by Louise and Aylmer Maude

Words & Idioms

beds: (n) an area in a garden where seeds are planted
execution: (n) the act of killing someone officially
hermit: (n) a man who lives alone in the wilderness, usually for religious reasons
property: (n) Usually the land, house, and animals that one owns
quit: (v) to leave or depart one's residence
seize: (v) to take something by force

Study Questions

1. Identify where Tolstoy uses irony in the story.

2. Write an essay where you apply the answers to the three questions to your own life.

3. How does understanding the answers to the three questions help one succeed in life?

4. This story can be considered a parable. "The Happy Prince" by Oscar Wilde can be called an allegory. First, define the difference between a parable and an allegory, and how each story fits into its genre.

5. Write a paper comparing and/or contrasting how these two stories relate to each other (if at all) and which one is more effective.

6. What is the significance of having the story be about a king? Would the story work just as well if it were a farmer or a knight? Why or why not?

Glossary

Allegory

A literary work in which the characters and their situations clearly represent general qualities and type-as, in an animal fable, each animal may represent a type of human personality. Often the characters of an allegory represent abstract vices or virtues such as avarice, charity, innocence, or prudery.

Ambiguity

Ambiguity refers to the fact that words can often have several meanings, thus creating uncertainty for the reader.

Archetype

An archetype is a basic model from which copies are made. It can be argued that at the heart of all works of literature are certain simple patterns that embody fundamental human concerns, the primary concern being the place of people in the natural world.

Ballad

Traditionally a popular, short folk tale created for the oral tradition, where a scop or Bard would sing, recite, or chant the tale. The "modern" literary ballad has been adapted from this earlier tradition.

Canon

Originally the term canon applied to the list of books in the Hebrew Bible and New Testament which was accepted by church authorities as genuine and having divine authority. Writings not admitted to the canon are called Apocrypha. The Protestant and Catholic churches differ as to which writings are apocryphal.

Character

The people in a novel are referred to as characters. We assess them on the basis of what the author tells us about them and on the basis of what they do and say. This is important: we must avoid loose conjecture about a character and establish everything from the evidence of the text. Another point to remember is that the characters are part of a broader pattern: they are members of a society, and the author's distinctive view of how people relate to society will be reflected in the presentation of every character. Details are not included just for their own sake but relate to the overall pattern of the novel.

Comic Novels

Novels primarily intended to make us laugh. Students are sometimes grudging in their praise of comic novels, as they can appear lightweight compared to realistic novels, which present such a substantial picture of life. A common, but misguided approach is to ascribe some social purpose to the writer and then to argue that the comedy makes the social criticism entertaining.

Contradiction

Contradiction occurs where we are faced with two or more meanings that cannot be reconciled or resolved. To this extent, it overlaps with ambiguity, but there are important differences. Critics tend to use ambiguity to demonstrate the richness of the texts being discussed. Contradiction, however, which has become a central term in poststructuralist criticism, points to incoherences or divisions in a text that undermine its apparent stability.

Gothic Novels

They concentrate on the more sensational side of romance; they depart from the social world, not to seek an ideal goal, but to explore the irrational passions of the mind.

Irony

Irony is a way of writing in which what is meant is contrary to what the words appear to say. Pope, for example, might praise someone extravagantly in his poetry, but the term used can be so extravagant that they signal to the reader that the person referred to does not deserve such praise.

Metaphor

A figure of speech in which one thing is described in terms of another. A simile is very nearly the same, but, whereas metaphor identifies one thing with another, a simile involves the notion of similarity, using the words 'like' or 'as.' Narrative is the organization of a series of events into the form of a story. This is obviously what we have in novels; what is less obvious is how similar the narrative structure is in most novels.

Narrative Structure

Narrative is the organization of a series of events into the form of a story. This is obviously what we have in novels; what is less obvious is how similar the narrative structure is in most novels.

Narrator

The narrator tells the story in a novel. Novels contain simple stories which, in their telling become complicated. There are two overlapping ways by which the novelist can complicate matters.

One is by introducing complications in the content: the inclusion of a mass of details about people, places, and events makes the story seem substantial and real. The other way in which the writer can complicate matters is by the way in which he or she chooses to narrate the story: a story can be told in many ways, for every narrator will see things from a different point-of-view.

Paradox

A paradox is a statement that appears to be contradictory or inconsistent with common sense though it may be quite true.

Pathetic Fallacy

It objects to the way in which poets attributed human feelings and actions to natural objects.

Plot

Plot is that framework of incidents, however simple or complex, upon which the narrative or drama is constructed, upon which the narrative or drama is constructed; the events of the depicted struggle, as organized into an artistic unit. The elements of plot are a beginning that presumes further action, a middle that presumes both previous and succeeding action, and an end that requires the preceding events but no succeeding action. The unity of the plot is thus the result of necessary relationship and order among the events, not that they center upon a single character.

Postmodernism

Like many of the 'post' terms of modem critical theory, postmodernism has a number of connected uses. In a literal sense, it refers to those works of art that were written after the modernist period of the early twentieth century, and whose style differs, often dramatically, from the previous modern style.

Realism

It is particularly associated with the nineteenth-century novel to refer to the idea that texts appear to represent 'the world' 'as it really is.' It means that they will select from their observations the material suitable for constructing a story that faithfully represents what they have understood. Realistic is the label we apply to those novels that seek to provide a convincing illusion of life as we normally think of it. Readers who are just beginning to study novels often feel most comfortable with realistic novels became they appear relatively straightforward. The realistic novel can seem like a clear window on the world—and as readers we can become fully involved with the characters and event—while non-realistic novels seem to look at the world through a distorting mirror with the result that we are forced to consider the relationship between the work of art itself and life.

Romance

We use the term 'romance' to describe those novels where the story is more adventurous or more fanciful than in realistic novels. Something grander than the novel's familiar concern with social issues is involved, for 'romance' suggests a search for some truth beyond that which we might encounter in ordinary experience. Both characters and events are removed from the everyday, so that there is always an air of the extraordinary about romance.

Satire

The humorous presentation of human folly or vice in such a way as to make it look ridiculous. The satirist aims to correct, by an exposure to ridicule, deviations from normal conduct or reasonable opinion. The chief tool of satire is to exaggerate deformities to the point at which their absurdity is unmistakably apparent.

Science Fiction (Sci-Fi)

The informing impulse can be to present a world where the problems of ordinary life are transcended and where the characters can live a more heroic or more ordered life, and ideas that are relevant today may be explored through metaphor to showcase the dramatic direction current thought is leading the world.

Stream of Consciousness Technique

A technique which seeks to record the random flow of impressions through a character's mind without any concern for form or convention.

Structure

The structure of a text is its overall shape and pattern. This is sometimes referred to as its form, though strictly speaking form is a more inclusive term which embraces every aspect of the work's technique.

Style

Style means the writers characteristic manner of expression. What in the end distinguishes one writer from another—so that the experienced reader could identify a passage as coming from, say, a Lawrence novel—is the style. Style changes from age to age, but every novelist has his or her own 'voice.'

Utopian Novel

A novel that presents a perfectly ordered society where all the problems of the real world have been eliminated. This is, however, more than simple day-dreaming: often the intention is that this should reflect back on the imperfections of the existing world.

INDEX

A

B

C

D

E

F

G

H

T

U

V

W

Oksun Kang 강옥선

부산대학교에서 박사학위를 받았으며, 동서대학교 영어학과 교수로 재직 중이다.

Steven Reeder 스티븐 리더

캘리포니아 주립대학에서 석사학위를 받았으며, 경성대학교 영어영문학과 교수로 재직 중이다.

Hyosun An 안효선(삽화 디자이너)

Academy of Art University, Fine Arts에서 석사학위를 받았으며, 이화여자대학교에서 박사학위를 받아, 이화여대 의류산업학과 전임연구원으로 재직 중이다.

Illustrated Short Stories in English

초판 1쇄 발행 _ 2017년 11월 30일

공 저 • 강 옥 선 · 스티븐 리더
발 행 인 • 정 현 걸
발 행 • 신 아 사
인 쇄 • 토탈프로세스
출판등록 • 1956년 1월 5일 (제9-52호)
주 소 • 서울시 은평구 통일로 59길 4(2층)
전 화 • 02)382-6411 · 팩스 02)382-6401
홈페이지 • www.shinasa.co.kr
E-MAIL • shinasa@daum.net

ISBN 978-89-8396-245-4(93840)

정가 13,000 원